WALKS IN
BERKSHIRE

WALKS IN
BERKSHIRE

 BERKSHIRE BOOKS

First published in 1992 by Berkshire Books

Copyright © 1992 Department of Highways and
Planning, Berkshire County Council

British Library Cataloguing in Publication Data

Countryside Walks in Berkshire
796.5

ISBN 0–7509–0150–0

BERKSHIRE BOOKS
Official Publisher to Berkshire County Council

Managed by
Alan Sutton Publishing Ltd
Phoenix Mill, Far Thrupp, Stroud,
Gloucestershire GL5 2BU
Tel: 0453 731114   Fax: 0453 731117

Typeset in 11pt Times.
Typesetting and origination by
Alan Sutton Publishing Limited.
Colour separation by Yeo Valley Reprographics.
Printed in Great Britain by
Bath Press Colour Books Ltd.

CONTENTS

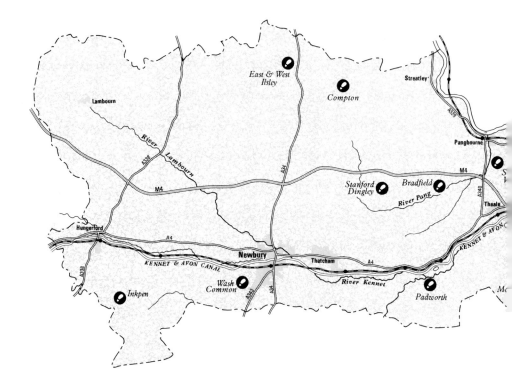

East & West
Ilsley

Lambourn

Compton

Streatley

A329

River Lambourn

A338

A34

Pangbourne

M4

Stanford
Dingley

Bradfield

River Pang

M4

A340

Theale

Hungerford

A4

KENNET & AVON

M4

A338

Newbury

KENNET & AVON CANAL

Thatcham

A4

River Kennet

Wash
Common

A343

A34

Padworth

Inkpen

0   5   16 kilometres

0   4   8   12   10 miles

Based upon the Ordnance Survey Map with the permission

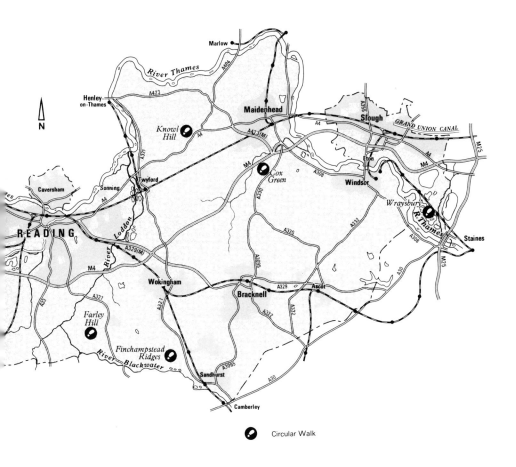

● Circular Walk

   Cartography by GEOprojects (U.K.) Ltd., Henley on Thames, Oxon.

This book has been compiled by staff of Berkshire County Council's Department of Highways and Planning, in particular Geoff Coles, Elaine Cox, Suzanne Hopes, Graham Walters and other members of the Rights of Way team, co-ordinated by Andrew Graham

PREFACE

This book brings together a series of circular walks in Berkshire which have been developed over recent years. In 1986 Berkshire County Council, with assistance from the Countryside Commission and the Manpower Services Commission, set up a project to identify, improve, and promote a series of routes which would be easy to use on foot, and in some cases on horseback. These routes would use the existing rights of way network, and would pass through interesting and attractive countryside. Such routes have been found to be effective ways of encouraging people into the countryside who are not confident about using rights of way.

After programmes of practical improvements including the installation of new stiles and gates, improved waymarking, vegetation clearance and path surfacing, the walks were promoted by the distribution of free leaflets, and the provision of map-boards at certain car parks. Gradually the walks have become widely known and popular so that there is less need to provide guidance on how to follow the routes. There is now the opportunity to tell walkers more about what they will see along the way. This book updates and adds to the information available in the original leaflets, and collects it all together under one cover.

As well as continuing to manage these circular walks, Berkshire County Council's Department of Highways and Planning also strives to maintain the rest of the rights of way network to an ever higher standard. Included in this will be maintenance of the Ridgeway National Trail, part of which passes through Berkshire, and the development of the Thames Path National Trail, both long-distance walking routes. Elsewhere, work continues to improve opportunities for horse riders and cyclists, and for those who prefer the challenge of a long walk, a 15-mile route linking the Ridgeway at White Horse Hill to the Kennet and Avon Canal towpath at Newbury is soon to be opened.

Any comments or observations which you may have upon the routes described in this book, and especially reports of any problems encountered when walking them, would be welcome and should be addressed to:

The Department of Highways and Planning,
Berkshire County Council,
Shire Hall,
Shinfield Park,
Reading,
Berkshire RG2 9XG

Telephone: Reading (0734) 234920

INTRODUCTION

The shape of the county's countryside

Berkshire offers some marvellously varied countryside for walking. The county's scenery results from the diverse underlying geology which shapes its hills and valleys, and ultimately influences the use to which man has put the land over the centuries. Although a detailed explanation of the county's geology and landform would easily fill a separate volume, a general understanding of it can add to the enjoyment of any walk in the countryside.

The Downs

The Berkshire Downs in the western half of the county form a distinctive landscape dominated by gently rolling and lightly folded hills, most of which are intensively used for arable farming, and where woodland cover is sparse. The Downs offer walks through open country with extensive views over neighbouring counties (East/West Ilsley and Compton walks). There are few villages to be found high on the Downs; most are located in the valleys in the chalk or on lower ground below (Inkpen walk).

There is also a southern extension of the Chilterns chalk into north-east Berkshire between Henley and Maidenhead which produces another attractive, slightly hilly landscape punctuated by a number of prominent hills formed by clay outcrops (Knowl Hill walk).

The River Valleys

Much of the county forms part of what is known as the London Basin, an extensive area of low ground bounded by the chalk uplands of the Berkshire Downs and the Chilterns to the north and the Hampshire Downs, the Hog's Back and the North Downs to the south. The basin is drained by the Thames and its tributaries, the most important of which in Berkshire is the Kennet. Off the chalk, the county is generally quite low-lying, the only significant features being the river valleys and higher land formed from remaining areas of plateau gravels.

The most significant river valley is clearly that of the Thames, although for the most part the river itself only forms a boundary to the county rather than flowing through it. Nonetheless, there are plenty of paths offering walks beside the wide waters of England's longest river (Wraysbury walk). By 1994 many of these paths will be linked together to form the Thames Path, a continuous walk between the Thames Barrier and the river's source in Gloucestershire. A river the size of the Thames produces a large flood plain of flat land. Although in places such as areas may be wet, especially in winter, they do provide gentle walking (Cox Green walk).

The next major river valley in the county is that of the Kennet, which stretches from the Thames at Reading westwards through Newbury and Hungerford and across the county boundary towards Marlborough. Altogether different from the Thames, the Kennet, fed by clear chalk streams and often dividing itself up into numerous lazily winding channels, flows through fertile and prosperous countryside. The newly re-opened Kennet and Avon Canal adds another feature of interest without detracting from the valley's beauty, while the towpath provides easy, level walking (Padworth walk).

A very much smaller river valley is that of the Pang, within the Area of Outstanding Natural Beauty west of Reading. Flanked by wooded hills and with a chain of charming villages down its length, the Pang Valley must be one of the most attractive parts of the county and one which is easy to explore along rights of way (Stanford Dingley, Bradfield and Sulham walks).

The Southern Plateaux

Stretching for almost the whole length of the county along its southern side is an intermittent ridge of higher ground, the tops of which are composed of gravels. These have produced distinctive landscapes and feature numerous areas of common land. While some of the area looks little different from the valleys below, the conifer plantations, heaths and birch woodlands create scenery rarely found elsewhere in the county. The commons are important sites for recreation. While some have numerous rights of way, others provide for general access by the public and most have become popular with local walkers (Wash Common, Mortimer, Farley Hill and Finchampstead walks).

THE WALKS – RIGHTS OF WAY AND ACCESS TO THE COUNTRYSIDE

The walks vary in length from 2 to 6 miles. Most offer the opportunity to take a brief walk by choosing a short-cut back to the start, while in the case of Mortimer and Sulham separate walks originating from the same point are offered. By combining these a walk of more than 6 miles is possible.

Apart from small sections of permitted path which have been agreed with the landowner, for the most part the routes in this book follow rights of way. These are highways which give the public the right to cross a piece of private land along a specified line. The right of way may be either a footpath, a bridleway, a byway, or a road used as a public path (RUPP). Each of these descriptions indicates that certain travellers may use them; for example, a bridleway may be used by walkers, those riding or leading a horse, or pedal cyclists. Although these different titles and definitions may seem a little daunting there is no need to worry as *all* are open to walkers and they have priority over other users. For this reason the route marked on the maps does not differentiate between the different types of path used.

To help people to make use of the rights of way network they are signposted from all metalled roads and extra signposting and waymarking is provided elsewhere in consultation with landowners. The routes in this book have been signposted and way-marked to a high standard to make them easy to follow. The arrows are of a standard size and design promoted by the Countryside Commission, and adopted throughout England and Wales. A nation-ally recognised colour coding system has been developed to show the status of the right of way indicated by the waymarkers. Yellow represents a footpath, blue a bridleway and red a byway. Gen-erally RUPPs are marked by blue arrows. The waymarkers and finger-posts indicating the circular routes described in this book are marked with the words RECREATION ROUTE in the centre of the arrow. At a junction where a number of rights of way meet, your way will be in the direction indicated by the RECREATION ROUTE sticker. As well as on the finger-posts these waymarkers will be found on gate posts, the uprights of stiles and bridge rails, and on specially provided wooden posts.

In many places a heavily trodden path across a field will indicate clearly which way to go, but elsewhere, where lush grass, recent vegetation man-agement or agricultural operations make it unclear, the waymarkers and signposts should be your guide. While every effort is taken to keep the routes in prime condition, there may be occasions, for exam-ple when rampant growth of brambles or grass obscures them, when the waymarkers need to be looked for. When the text indicates that your course turns off to the left or right, keep your eyes open so as not to miss the waymarkers.

ADDITIONAL INFORMATION

Information provided in the text on public transport, refreshments, etc., is as up to date as possible but may be subject to change, so it is impossible to guarantee its accuracy. In some cases the walks start from large car parks, but others rely on small roadside parking areas. Although it is unlikely that large numbers of people will be walking the same route simultaneously it is still important to park carefully and considerately, especially in villages. If you plan to walk one of the routes in a large party it would be advisable to visit beforehand to check whether there will be sufficient parking for your needs.

Bee Line Bus Company produces a bus timetable booklet for the following areas: Reading; Newbury; Bracknell and Windsor; Maidenhead and Slough. These detail Bee Line services and also those provided by other operators. Berkshire County Council produces 'Connections' – bus and train timetables for Slough.

Although the signposts and waymarks on the ground and the combination of the notes and maps in the text should enable you to follow these routes with ease, you may find that a good Ordnance Survey map of the area will add to your enjoyment. The great majority of Berkshire is covered by just two Landranger maps (with magenta covers) at a scale of 1:50,000. These are ideal for deciding a route from home to the start of a walk, or to get ideas for other places to visit. To get a more detailed picture of the countryside around you the Pathfinder Series of maps (with green covers) at a scale of 1:25,000 will be more helpful. These are clearly marked with a huge amount of detail, including the rights of way network, at a scale which makes them quite easy to use. To achieve full coverage of the county with Pathfinders requires the purchase of fourteen maps, but if you build up your collection gradually as you explore new parts of the county you will end up with a very valuable reference.

No part of Berkshire can be considered remote from civilisation like some of the hill-walking country of Wales, northern England or Scotland. Nonetheless, high on the Downs, in poor winter weather, the comforting shelter of Compton or East Ilsley can seem an awfully long walk away. Your appreciation of the Ridgeway's ancient splendour can be somewhat diminished if you are being battered by horizontal sleet while wearing little more than a T-shirt, shorts and trainers. It is important therefore to consider your clothing, especially foot-wear, and how long the walk is going to take, before you set out. With a little thought about whether you need to take food and drink and waterproofs with you, and a check of the weather forecast before you set out, there is no reason why anyone should encounter any real difficulties on these routes.

The problem you are most likely to encounter is that of mud; however prone to drought we become, a bout of wet weather still manages to turn some parts of the countryside to sticky, clinging gunge.

And of course, in places you will walk through farms or fields used by cattle or horses, and these areas may become very mucky in winter. It's all a part of the countryside, though, and shouldn't pose a problem so long as you've thought ahead and worn suitable boots.

THE COUNTRY CODE

Although all of the paths followed on the routes in this book follow either rights of way or permitted paths, you will for the most part be crossing private land. It is especially important therefore to keep in mind the spirit of the Country Code. On these walks you may stop and rest or take refreshment, provided that you stay on the path and do not cause damage or obstruction. Landowners and their managers seldom object to members of the public enjoying the countryside if they cause no harm and create no problems or disturbance. Remember that it often only takes one unfortunate incident to colour a farmer's view of all walkers crossing his land. Try to be considerate and ensure that no careless or thoughtless act on your or your party's behalf causes an incident which may make the countryside less welcoming to future visitors.

You may take your dog with you, provided it is kept on a lead or is otherwise effectively controlled, remains on the path and does not 'worry' livestock. It is illegal to have a dog off the lead or not under close control in a field where there are sheep, as is the case on a number of these walks.

The Country Code is not meant to be a set of

rules. It is to help countryside visitors to appreciate the problems they may inadvertently cause. During your walks bear these points in mind:

Enjoy the countryside and respect its life and work
Guard against all risks of fire
Fasten all gates
Keep your dogs under proper control
Keep to the public paths across farmland
Use gates and stiles to cross fences, hedges and walls
Leave livestock, crops and machinery alone
Take your litter home
Help to keep all water clean
Protect wildlife, plants and trees
Take special care on country roads
Make no unnecessary noise

AERIAL PHOTOS

Berkshire County Council's Department of Highways and Planning regularly commissions an aerial photographic survey of the county. The latest, taken during the summer of 1991, has been used to provide a unique view of the landscapes through which the walks in this book pass. We become so used to observing our countryside from head height, or from the seat of a moving car, that just taking a ride along country lanes on the top of a double-decker bus can be a revelation. The views from the air provide a massive change in perspective and scope. By looking at the countryside from above in this way it is possible to see the way that different elements in the landscape lie in relation to one another, how settlements and farms are located in relation to lines of communication or sources of water, and to spot features invisible from roads and footpaths.

Each walk description is accompanied by an aerial view of all or part of the walk. The extent of the photo's coverage is marked on the appropriate route map. We suggest that you refer to the photo as you walk. In winter this will give you a chance to visualise how the area looks in summer, but at any time of year it should help to give you a feel for the wider landscape through which you travel. It will also show you how some of the features you see, for example rivers, woods or farmland, take their place in a wider pattern of the landscape, and how each may contribute greatly to the look of the countryside in some parts of the county while being insignificant elsewhere.

The photos also emphasise the difference between the countryside found in different parts of the county. Although some parts may seem superficially similar to the walker, the wider view from the air can reveal great disparities in size between fields, or considerable differences between the shape, size and composition of the woodlands found in separate areas. The contrast between the ways that villages have developed is also notable. In some, all the houses are tightly grouped around a central well, pond, or road, while in others cottages and farmhouses are scattered along lanes and roads over a wide area and have only come to be called a village for convenience's sake. All this variety is a result of a complex land-use history and the ebb and flow in the fortunes of Berkshire's countryside, its industries, its people, and their livelihoods. This typically English variety of scene and detail is what makes the countryside such a fascinating place to explore. The rights of way network which covers the whole county offers an opportunity to do just that.

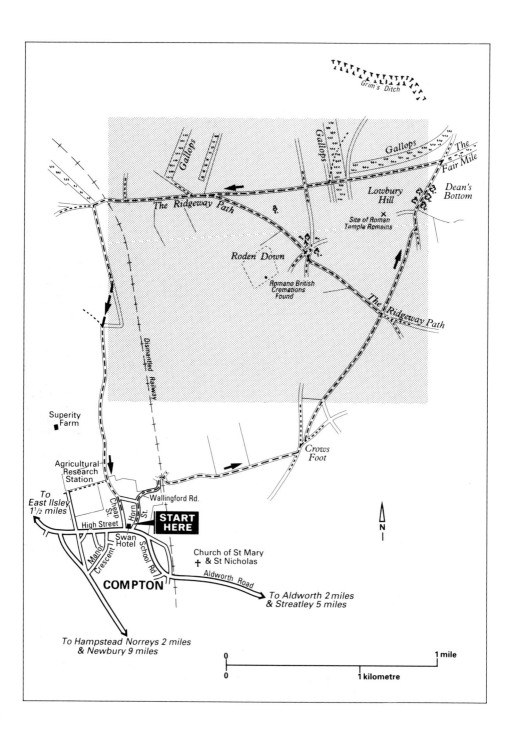

Grim's Ditch

Gallops

Gallops

Gallops

The Fair Mile

Lowbury Hill

Dean's Bottom

The Ridgeway Path

Site of Roman Temple Remains

Roden Down

Romano British Cremations Found

The Ridgeway Path

Dismantled Railway

Superity Farm

Agricultural Research Station

Crows Foot

To East Ilsley 1½ miles

Wallingford Rd.

Cheap St.

Horn St.

START HERE

High Street

Swan Hotel

Manor Crescent

School Rd.

Church of St Mary & St Nicholas

Aldworth Road

COMPTON

To Aldworth 2 miles & Streatley 5 miles

To Hampstead Norreys 2 miles & Newbury 9 miles

N

0   1 mile

0   1 kilometre

WALK ONE:
COMPTON

6 MILES

The high country of the Berkshire Downs has few landmarks. Only the clusters of trees at Roden Clump punctuate the sweep of these rolling croplands, while farm tracks and the winding Ridgeway trace chalk lines across the hillsides.

INTRODUCTION

The route is about 6 miles long and should take about $3\frac{1}{2}$ hours to do on foot. The route has been described in an anti-clockwise direction from the Swan Hotel in Compton, and may be used by horseriders as well as walkers.

The village of Compton is on the Berkshire Downs, and its origins stretch back to before the Domesday Book. The remains of an Iron Age hill-fort lie about a mile south of the village: called Perborough Castle, it was one of a series of hill-forts close to the Ridgeway. Compton was fully recorded in the Domesday Book, and at that time had two manors. Both fell into the hands of supporters of William the Conqueror. Over time, one manor (house and farms) came into the possession of the Lloyd family; land and farms were later sold to sitting tenants.

Today's village is an interesting blend of old and new. The picturesque cottages are huddled round the centre of the village close to the Swan Hotel. The newer dwellings on the outskirts of the village are only a short walk from the church of St Mary and St Nicholas. The tower is thirteenth-century, and the font is of twelfth-century origin. During the Reformation much of the church was destroyed, and what we see today is the result of years of rebuilding and constant restoration. The bell-tower contains six bells: these were cast in 1775 by Pack and Chapman of London.

THE WALK

Start by going up Horn Street and turn right into Wallingford Road. Follow the road until the old railway bridge is reached.

During the early 1880s a railway was built with the intention of linking the Great Western Railway's line at Didcot with the London and South Western Region Railway's line at Southampton. Such a north-south route, offering a link from the important south coast port up towards the industrial heartland of the Midlands, appeared to be a good proposition. However, the Didcot, Newbury and Southampton Junction Railway, as the enterprise was called, soon ran into difficulties. The line was built to GWR specifications, the deep cuttings carved through the downs reflecting the GWR's obsession with minimal gradients. The cost of this work was far out of proportion to the likely profits which the line would show and eventually funds ran out. The DNSJR was forced into an agreement with the LSWR in order to survive, and the line eventually became part of the great GWR network.

Compton station served the villages of Aldworth, East and West Ilsley and Compton. The station could handle much horse-box traffic by way of special sidings, but its most important trade was in sheep going to and from the Ilsley sheep fairs. Pens were erected in the station sidings to hold animals in transit. Following a post-war drop in passenger traffic and the decline of the wool industry in the 1960s, the railway closed; the lines were taken up in 1967.

Pass under the railway bridge and turn right onto a bridleway which runs between two hedges.

Such unsurfaced tracks, bounded by hedges and verges and often of great age, are frequently referred to as 'green lanes'. This term has no legal status, although the green lanes followed on this route are mostly public rights of way. These arose as a result of nineteenth-century Enclosure Acts in which common land was split up into individually owned parcels, the rights of way usually running between them. Indeed the boundaries of the parcels of land may have been determined by the tracks, which may already have been very old.

Follow the green lane gently uphill towards the next large track junction. Turn left here and after a short distance turn right and then left onto the track which makes up the central 'claw' of this junction which, as a glance at the map will show, is aptly named Crow's Foot.

This track is one of many which run up to the top of the Downs from the villages and hamlets that lie on either side. Many of these tracks have been in use for centuries as a means of access to the Ridgeway, and indicate its past importance. The Ridgeway track is steeped in history and tradition. It starts at Ivinghoe Beacon in Buckinghamshire and follows the chalk

The Ridgeway on
remote Roden Down

ridge to Overton Hill in Wiltshire, a distance of
85 miles. Other routes have been identified which
linked to the coast in Dorset and North Norfolk. The
age of the Ridgeway is uncertain. Some say the track
is England's oldest road, possibly dating to the
Bronze Age some 3,000 years ago. Neolithic man
chose the dry chalk hills for woodland clearance and
subsequent grazing with domesticated animals. The
short springy turf which we associate with chalk
downlands may date from these times. By the
Bronze Age the Ridgeway may have been an important trading route. Later, fortifications on and near

27

the Ridgeway were constructed, Perborough Castle south of Compton being a local example. The Roman invaders found these forts a serious resistance. In time, more efficient iron tools allowed the clearance of trees for farmland lower in the valleys and the higher downland tracks became less frequented, although they remained important as drove roads.

The path reaches the Ridgeway where five tracks converge. Here you have the choice of two routes. Turn left onto the Ridgeway for the shorter route, or go straight across for the route around Lowbury Hill.

Once called Lowborough Hill, Lowbury Hill commands one of the finest views from the Ridgeway. The remains of a Roman temple were discovered on the summit, along with a Roman military outpost. From Lowbury Hill, twelve other entrenchments occupied by Roman forces were visible. To the east of Lowbury the land falls away sharply, forming a deep valley known as Dean's Bottom.

Beyond Lowbury Hill the route reaches another major track junction. The track on the right is called 'The Fair Mile'. This was set out in Aston Tirrold's Enclosure award of 1743, when it was 132 ft wide. It runs from this junction north-eastwards to the A417 at the foot of the Downs near Moulsford.

Turn left.

This track, which connects the Fair Mile with the Ridgeway, runs alongside some training gallops, and also crosses a gallop at one point. Keep to the right

The Ridgeway at
Roden Clump

of way and should you meet any, treat the racehorses
with great respect. Below the Ridgeway, on the
north face of the Downs, runs a part of Grims Ditch.
This intermittent earthwork is thought to have been
dug as a boundary between ancient tribal territories
in the North Berkshire Downs and the Vale of the
White Horse. Its date is uncertain; some parts are
prehistoric, while others are more recent.

**Follow the track until it meets the shorter route at the
Ridgeway. Continue west along the Ridgeway.**

On the left and slightly below can be seen Roden
Down. The land around Roden Down was farmed in
the Iron Age. Signs of this ancient agriculture still
survive in the form of dykes and ditches. After the
Roman invasion of AD 43 the land around Rowden
became a cemetery. Over the years, fragments of
pottery, human bones and a multitude of coins have
been discovered, thrown up during cultivation.
Although such signs of past cultivation do exist,

29

because the chalkland soils are so thin, apart from the times of agricultural boom most of the Downs have been vast areas of uninterrupted sheep pasture. Since food imports could not be relied upon during the Second World War, large areas of sheep pasture were ploughed up for the first time to produce wheat, barley and oats. Since then we have grown accustomed to seeing the Downs under crops, and only small patches of the rich downland turf remain.

The Ridgeway itself represents an important linear nature reserve. Its turf, hedges and verges remain undisturbed compared to the cropped fields all around, and contain numerous plants and insects not found elsewhere. The chalkland soil, being shallow and well drained, warms up quickly after rain. The lack of nutrients prevents any one plant from taking over to the detriment of others, and some particularly rich sites may have dozens of plant species within a small area. Plants adapted to life in a dry, exposed, chalk grassland – able to withstand grazing, wind, drought, and lime-rich soil – are a speciality here, as are the insects which feed upon them.

The route recrosses the disused railway line and at the next junction turns left down a bridleway. The bridleway initially runs down a horse-trainer's private chalk road before turning right to cross an arable field. The bridleway then runs alongside the chalk road and ends at the metalled road at the northern end of the village.

To your right is the Compton Agricultural Research Station which studies animal diseases. Other agricultural research stations have been responsible for breeding new barley varieties which can grow on the shallow soils of the Downs. The use of these varieties has allowed the conversion of the sheep pastures to arable land.

Follow the road down and turn right into Cheap Street: this will take you to the end of the route.

HOW TO GET THERE

By Car

There is no obvious and direct route to Compton. The best way to avoid getting lost in the cobweb of small lanes and tracks in the countryside north-east of Newbury is to approach the village via East Ilsley. Take the A34 north from Newbury and turn off into East Ilsley. Drive through the village following directions to Compton, which lies a couple of miles to the east.

By Bus

Bennett's Coach service B34 between Newbury and West Ilsley runs via Compton. On Saturday the service is extended to and from Oxford. Tel. Chieveley (0635) 248423.

REFRESHMENTS

The Swan Hotel in the centre of the village.

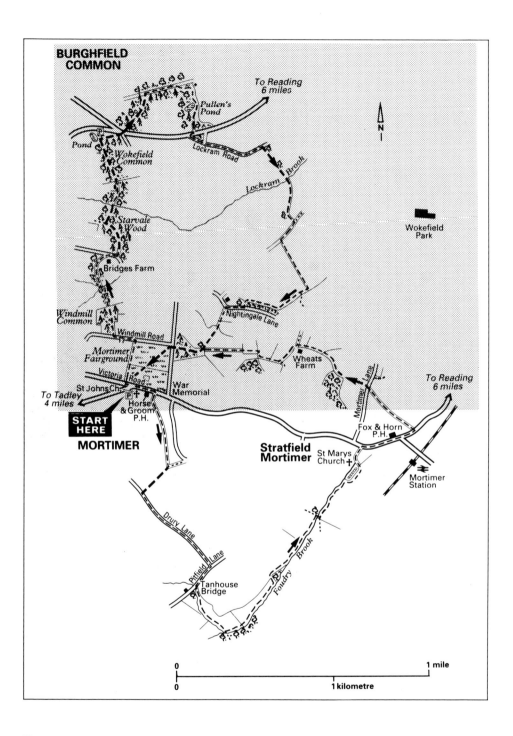

BURGHFIELD COMMON

To Reading 6 miles

N

Pullen's Pond

Pond

Wokefield Common

Lockram Road

Lockram Brook

Wokefield Park

Starvale Wood

Bridges Farm

Nightingale Lane

Windmill Common

Windmill Road

Mortimer Fairground

Wheats Farm

Victoria Road

Mortimer Lane

To Reading 6 miles

St Johns Ch.

War Memorial

To Tadley 4 miles

Horse & Groom P.H.

Fox & Horn P.H.

START HERE

MORTIMER

Stratfield Mortimer

St Marys Church

Mortimer Station

Drury Lane

Foudry Brook

Pitfield Lane

Tanhouse Bridge

0		1 mile
0		1 kilometre

WALK TWO:
MORTIMER

3 MILES

Although always close to the nearby villages, the dense tree cover of the common combined with the thick farmland hedgerows almost makes the walker feel he is journeying through a large and remote forest.

INTRODUCTION

Two contrasting walks are described for the Mortimer area. They comprise a northern and a southern loop and both are described from a start point at the Fairground at Mortimer. Each walk is about 3 miles long and each should take about 2 hours. The northern walk runs mainly through one of the county's numerous commons, a dry area of birch and oak woodland and pine plantations criss-crossed by paths. In contrast, the southern walk runs through open agricultural land following some of the numerous streams which flow towards the River Kennet.

THE WALKS

Northern Walk through Wokefield Common

Walk north along the left-hand side of the Fairground.

The large square of open land known as Mortimer Fairground was dedicated for public use when the area was subject to enclosure (the turning of communal open fields into individually owned holdings) in

1805. The furze and heath which covered the common then, has today given way to an area of well-kept grassland. In the nineteenth century the annual horse and cattle fairs must have been important events in the calendar of this then comparatively isolated village. Stock traders would have travelled far to attend the fair and would have brought news, gossip and novelty to the villagers. The Welsh horse-traders clearly made an impact during their stays – Welshman's Road in the village is named after them. The fairs have now been replaced by the occasional visit from circus troupes and funfairs.

On reaching Windmill Road turn left. Walk about 200 yards and turn right onto the footpath at the end of Windmill Court. This path crosses Windmill Common.

This common is so called because in the eighteenth century the Revd James Morgan arranged for a windmill and cottage to be built here. On this high land, at a time when the landscape was dominated by low-growing heath and scrub, this may not have been such a bad idea. However, with the 1804 Enclosure Act the land passed back to the lord of the manor, who planted the common with conifers. In 1832 the owner of the windmill wrote, 'It lays under the necessity to remove because the fir plantation has overgrown and keep the wind off the mill'. By 1937 the mill had gone, and all that remains are some of the offending conifers.

On leaving the conifers the walk follows a track across a small valley with a stream at its bottom.

This track is probably quite old, as is indicated by its slightly sunken nature and by the banks with hedges on either side. In time, tracks on soft soil and slopes gradually get lower owing to erosion. Before reaching the road by Bridges Farm, a ditch and bank with old beech trees can be seen to the left of the track. Ditches and banks with old trees are often old boundary markers – look out for further examples as you continue your walk.

Turn right onto the road at the farm, and shortly afterwards turn left onto the next. Follow this until it joins a bridleway and here turn right. This bridleway goes through Starvale Wood and passes by a house before entering Wokefield Common.

This is one of a number of commons found along the ridge of higher ground between Reading and Newbury, south of the Kennet valley. They are remnants of a land use pattern from the Middle Ages. Then, after the better land had been taken into cultivation to produce crops for the local manor, what was left remained as waste and was used for grazing or as a source of fuel by the cottagers. The right to do so was recognised in the courts, so the lord of the manor was unable to enclose these commons – split them up into private fields by planting hedges – without the authority of Parliament. However, during the great enclosure movement of the nineteenth century large expanses of these wastes were enclosed, and the commons we find today are all that remain of originally much larger areas.

Occupying poor gravelly soils, and constantly grazed or cleared of anything which could be used for firewood, the wastes were aptly named. Often bleak and barren places, the resort of robbers or social outcasts, commons were sometimes threatening places. Today, years since grazing ceased and after considerable amounts of tree-planting, the commons present an entirely different scene. Where areas of heather and furze have managed to survive they are important wildlife habitats providing homes for plants and insects not found elsewhere. Unfortunately, few such patches remain in Wokefield Common. Some commons still have commoners' rights. These are rights which certain registered people, usually the owners of specific properties – the rights being associated with the property rather than the person – may exercise on the common even though they do not own it. These rights are most often to graze stock, although rights to dig turf or collect firewood do exist. On Wokefield Common there is no public right of access apart from along the rights of way. However, under a management scheme established between the landowner and Newbury District Council, inhabitants of the district and neighbourhood are allowed to use this area, and numerous paths and tracks have been developed.

Follow the waymarks across the common. At the large pond the walk bears right and leads to a road junction. Cross the road and take the bridleway opposite. Follow the bridleway, passing a small pond on the left, and at the next large track turn right. This track takes the walk through the wood, which is mainly planted with oak and other broadleaved trees. The track bears right by a house and passes Pullen's Fish Pond before emerging at a road.

Pullen's Fish Pond is clearly man-made; the walk takes you across the dam which contains its waters. Ponds such as this were probably used to stock fish for use in nearby great houses of the past. Today they represent important wildlife sites, as the number of natural lakes and ponds in the countryside has dwindled rapidly.

At the road turn right, then go immediately left towards Wokefield at the road junction. Walk down Lockram Road, and after passing Lockram Farmhouse turn right into a field onto a footpath which runs down to Lockram Brook.

You have crossed Lockram Brook once before on this walk, near Bridges Farm close to the spring which is its source. There are a number of small brooks and streams in the area fed by springs formed where the porous gravel beds meet the impervious clay. All these streams eventually flow into the Foundry Brook and thence to the Kennet on the southern edge of Reading.

Cross the brook: the path follows the field boundary up the hill, passing through a small parcel of uncultivated land. Cross the stile at the top of the hill and turn right along the track. Turn left at the next field boundary and walk down the field edge to the stile.

While you are walking down this path take time to look at the view. The wide expanse of the flat agricultural clay plain to the east contrasts with the higher, often wooded ground of Mortimer and Wokefield Common to the west. Wokefield Park can be seen on the left. This was originally built for the Palmer family, then it became a school, but it is now a conference centre.

Cross the stile. The path follows another small stream and then the edge of a copse. At the end of the copse, turn left, to reach Nightingale Lane. Turn right along the lane for a short distance before turning left at the next footpath sign. Follow the path across two fields to the wood.

Here the Southern Walk joins the Northern Walk. Continue through the wood to emerge at a road opposite the top corner of the Fairground. Walk diagonally across the Fairground to the end of the northern walk.

The Southern Walk along Foudry Brook

From the Fairground, walk east down Victoria Road passing the school and the Horse and Groom public house. Take the footpath on the right, which runs down beside a house, then bears left between the gardens, before opening out to follow the backs of some more houses. The path then crosses a field to end at Drury Lane. Turn left down this lane.

This part of the walk offers fine views. You are walking along a part of the gravel plateau, the higher ground upon which Mortimer and Wokefield Common are situated. You should be able to see other parts of the plateau which form the high ground in the area. In many cases these are now clothed in woodland.

At the T-junction, turn right into Pitfield Lane. Walk down this lane to Tanhouse Bridge. Just before the bridge turn left onto a footpath. This footpath runs down the side of West End Brook on its way to join Foudry Brook.

Just a little upstream from this point the Roman Road between Staines (*Pontes*) and Silchester (*Calleva*) crossed the Foudry Brook. This was an important route and is still visible in places. Its line has been preserved by present-day footpaths, bridleways and, in places, roads. The Road acquired the local name of the Devil's Highway, the devil often in the past being blamed for something of unknown origin. The Roman Road is responsible for the local place-name Stratfield. This was originally Stradfield, which meant 'open land traversed by a Roman Road'. You are currently in the parish of Stratfield Mortimer, while to the south are the villages of Stratfield Saye and Stratfield Turgis. The remains of the Roman town of Calleva, including its walls and excavated amphitheatre, are just south-west of here and are well worth a visit, as is the tiny museum in Silchester village.

At the junction of West End Brook and Foudry Brook, turn left.

Apart from the railway traffic, to which wildlife becomes accustomed quite rapidly, this is a tranquil area. The waterside along Foudry Brook is always a good place to watch out for water birds such as grey wagtails, kingfishers and grey herons. The quieter you are, the more likely you are to see wildlife.

Walking across open fields on the edge of Mortimer

Follow Foudry Brook across three fields, then cross the brook at a footbridge. The path runs along the opposite bank and finishes at a stile. Cross the stile and a bridge and walk up the drive to St Mary's Church.

The present St Mary's was erected under the patronage of the lord of the manor, John Benyon, in 1866. However, its Victorian aspect reveals only a small part of the church's historical interest. Believed to be the fifth church on the site, the original St Mary's probably dates from Norman times. Behind the organ stands a stained glass window composed in part of glass from the original Norman building.

Follow the drive down to the road and turn right, passing the Fox and Horn public house. Turn left at the next road junction. The right-hand turning leads to Mortimer Station.

Mortimer Station is one of the few remaining examples of Brunel's original designs.

After passing the last house, take the path on the left which leads up to Mortimer Lane. Cross the lane, and take the path opposite, which leads to Wheat's Farm. Pass between the farm buildings and up to a track. Cross the track and go through the gate to turn left at the footpath sign. Follow the path around the edge of this field, crossing the stiles where it has now been set out into paddocks. The path leaves the field at a stile to run for a short distance along another field before crossing another stile. Then it runs between a hedge and a fence to end at the wood. Here the southern walk meets the northern walk.

Follow the waymarks through the wood to emerge at the Fairground. Walk diagonally across the Fairground and you have reached the end of the walk. Alternatively, you can walk down the road to your left to the War Memorial.

The War Memorial, which was designed by Herbert Maryon, a sculptor at University College in Reading, is made of Portland stone with gilded bronze plaques. It was unveiled on 9 October 1921. It is one of two monuments to fifty-six men of Mortimer who lost their lives in the 1914–18 war. The other is the football pitch which was cleared from the wilderness of furze on the Common by the Garth Club.

HOW TO GET THERE

By Car

Although it is quite a large village, Mortimer is never easy to find for the newcomer. It has to be approached through the maze of minor roads which lies to the south-west of Reading. It is well signposted, however, from the A33 at Three Mile Cross or Riseley. There is a car-parking area in front of the church on the south side of the Fairground.

By Bus

The Bee Line Bus Company service No. 143 between Reading and Tadley stops at Mortimer (Monday to Saturday). Tel. Reading 581358 for timetable information. Hampshire Bus service 153 between Basingstoke, Tadley, Burghfield and Reading via Mortimer on Sundays. Tel. (0256) 464501 for timetable details.

By Train

British Rail run a service between Reading and Basingstoke stopping at Mortimer. Tel. Reading 595911 or Basingstoke 464966.

REFRESHMENTS

Horse and Groom public house in Mortimer and the Fox and Horn public house at Stratfield Mortimer.

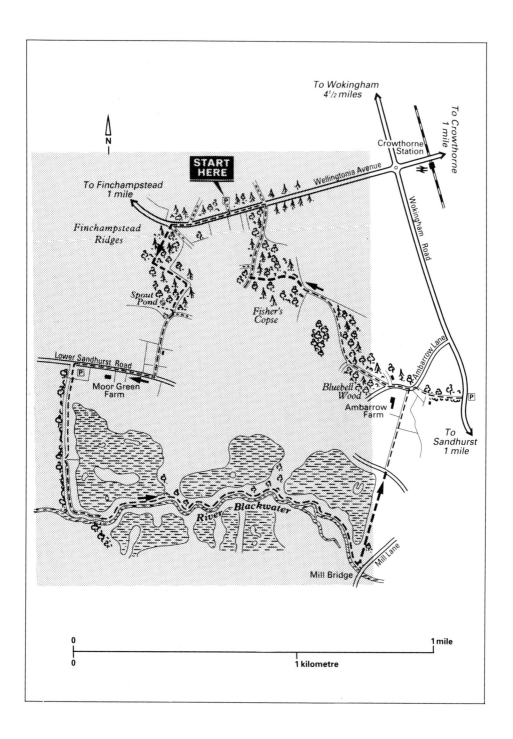

WALK THREE:
FINCHAMPSTEAD RIDGES

3 MILES

Man has made his mark on this landscape. Gravel pits, working or restored, fill the valley bottom, and alter the scene for ever. Just as remarkable but less intrusive is the line drawn by Wellingtonia Avenue on the Ridges.

INTRODUCTION

The walk is about $3\frac{1}{2}$ miles long and should take about $2\frac{1}{2}$ hours. It passes through an attractive area, combining a wooded ridge and a wide valley. Gravel extraction has altered the landscape, but as a result of cooperation between the gravel company, Halls Aggregates, and Berkshire County Council, the land has been restored for the benefit of wildlife, and extra public access has been provided. The walk follows public rights of way and also some 'permitted paths', with the agreement of the landowners. The route has been described in an anti-clockwise direction from the National Trust car park at Wellingtonia Avenue.

THE WALK

From the National Trust car park walk back down the drive to the road (Wellingtonia Avenue).

The National Trust, set up over ninety years ago, is the second largest landowner in the country (after the Crown) and its origins are based very firmly in landscape and wildlife conservation. Its objectives include promoting the permanent preservation of land for the benefit of the nation, with special reference to the preservation of its natural aspect, features, and animal and plant life. Most of the Trust's properties are open to the public at all times.

In 1863 John Walters, MP, of Bear Wood Estate, constructed this road over the Ridges. It was planted in 1869 with Wellingtonia trees. Some of the tallest trees in the world have been Wellingtonias (*Sequoiadendron giganteum*). They can grow to over 350 ft, weigh 1,000 tons and may live for 4,000 years in their native habitat, the western slopes of the Sierra Nevada in California. In Europe they will grow on average to 160 ft high and will probably live for about 1,000 years. Though these examples at Wellingtonia Avenue are less than 150 years old, they are already an impressive feature which dominates the scene. The bark of these trees is very thick and soft compared with the bark of our native pine. The cones can stay on the tree for about twenty years before they drop.

Turn right along the road, and cross to the other side, before turning left into the open spaces of Finchampstead Ridges.

Finchampstead Ridges (The National Trust) attracts large numbers of visitors. The hilltop consists of a considerable cap of plateau gravel which produces very poor soils. In the late twelfth and early thirteenth centuries this area was part of Windsor Forest, which at that time covered a considerable part of Berkshire. When the Forest contracted in size, the poor soils of this area made it less attractive for agriculture and so it remained as either woodland or heath. The strip of open heather remaining beside the road is a small remnant of what would have previously been a greater expanse. The Ridges are famed for the fine views over the Blackwater Valley, but today the woodland which has sprung up on the heath is nearly obscuring them. The whole of the Ridges are open for informal walking.

Follow the waymarked path down through the wood to a large track.

As you follow the path through these woods keep a close watch on the vegetation growing beside the path. As well as those plants associated with the dry sandy soils you would expect on the gravel, there are damp areas which hold entirely different groups of species. In places where the water seepage out of the ground is particularly bad it has been necessary to put in drains to keep the paths from becoming waterlogged. These damp, acid soils can be particularly rewarding places in which to search for fungi in autumn.

Before passing out of the wood onto the track, look to your right, where you will see Spout Pond, again interesting for the plants and animals which can thrive in the acidic conditions of its waters.

Turn right down the track and at the road (Lower Sandhurst Road), turn right. Walk past Moor Green Farm, and turn into the car park on the left. Take the footpath which runs down towards the lake from the car park.

This footpath runs alongside a new bridleway which provides a link to Moulsham Green in Hampshire.

Bluebell Wood

The path and bridleway are largely separated by a fence and hedge, and lead to the River Blackwater.

In common with other river valleys in Berkshire, that of the Blackwater River is underlain by important gravel deposits. Over time much gravel has been extracted, but in recent years, since the development of planning laws, the work has been carried out in a controlled manner, the active pits gradually moving down the valley. At present this is the furthest point that gravel working has progressed westwards on the Berkshire side of the valley.

The three flooded gravel pits on the left have been restored for nature conservation and are managed by the Berkshire, Buckinghamshire and Oxfordshire Naturalists' Trust (BBONT). Gravel extraction ceased in 1989, but well before that plans for the restoration of the land had been drawn up. Native trees and shrubs, such as willow, alder, field maple, hawthorn and hazel, have been planted around the lakes' margins. Some areas have been reseeded as wildflower meadows, and in places reed beds will be established at the water's edge.

While the gravel was being dug, the pits would have been pumped dry. Before the pits were flooded at the end of the process, islands were formed, some capped with gravel to encourage nesting terns, others designed so as to draw loafing ducks and geese. A bank has also been created in the hope that sandmartins will nest. To minimise disturbance, public access is being restricted to the meadow along the western side of the north-west lake and to two viewing hides which will be built shortly.

BBONT is a voluntary organisation which promotes wildlife conservation by acquiring and managing nature reserves (of which the trust has over ninety) and increasing public awareness of wildlife in the countryside. BBONT also provides advice on nature conservation to various bodies.

Finchampstead Ridges in the distance rise above the Blackwater Valley

Follow the footpath along the Blackwater River to the wooden bridge. Here the bridleway crosses over into Hampshire, but the walk continues on the Berkshire side of the river using the newly-created riverside footpath.

The Blackwater River flows in a north-westerly direction in a shallow valley between Farnham and Eversley before joining the River Loddon south-east of Reading. There is a long-term aim to provide a riverside walk along the whole length of the Blackwater Valley, stretching from the rather urban parts of the valley near Farnborough and Camberley to the quiet rural reach near Eversley. By negotiation with sympathetic landowners, and by obtaining

51

The wooded slopes of Finchampstead Ridges.

new sections of path from gravel companies when they are restoring worked sites, the pieces of the route are gradually falling into place.

Just before the path reaches the gate at Mill Bridge turn left and follow the waymarked path across open land beside a lake to a road. Cross the road and follow the path up the hill to Ambarrow Lane. (The path from the Ambarrow Court car park joins the route from the right here.)

Ambarrow Farm at the top of the lane is an attractive Victorian composition of a three-storey brick and stone farmhouse with a group of red brick and tile farm buildings. Its situation is unique within this part of the valley, being located on a steep-sided promontory with a commanding view over the meadows backed by the woodland to the north.

Turn left down the lane past the farm, then right onto the track through Bluebell Wood. The path bears right at the end of the wood and runs gently uphill to enter Fishers Copse. Follow the waymarks through the copse, turning right on to the wide track, and follow it back to Wellingtonia Avenue. Turn left along the road to the car park.

HOW TO GET THERE

By Car

The Wellingtonia Avenue car park is on the right-hand side of the B3348 half way between Finchampstead village and Crowthorne. Alternative car parking can be found adjacent to Moor Green Farm on the Lower Sandhurst Road south of Finchampstead Ridges, and at Ambarrow Court, only a short walk from the circular route, on the A321 just north of Sandhurst.

By Bus

The Bee Line Bus Company service No. 193

The Blackwater Valley path as it follows the river away from Mill Lane

between Reading, Wokingham, Crowthorne and Camberley (Monday to Saturday), stops by the roundabout at Wellingtonia Avenue, Crowthorne. Tel. Reading 581358 for timetable information.

By Train

British Rail run a service between Reading and Guildford stopping at Crowthorne Station which is a short stroll down the Wellingtonia Avenue from the walk. Tel. Reading 595911 for timetable information.

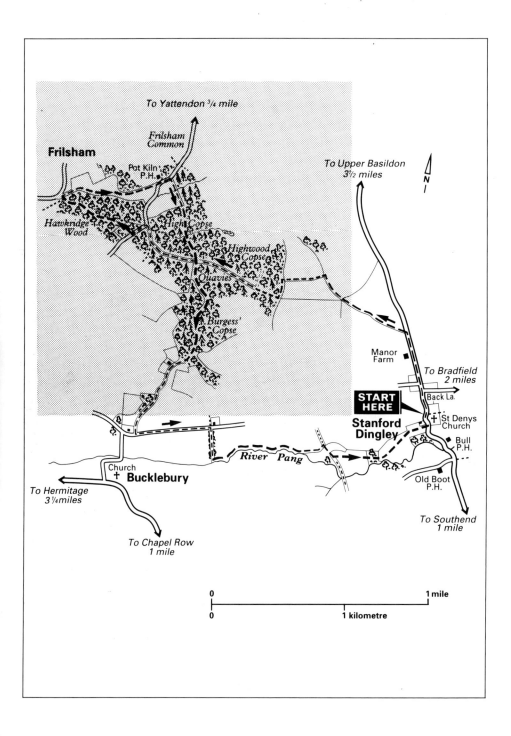

To Yattendon ¾ mile

Frilsham Common

Frilsham

Pot Kiln P.H.

Hawkridge Wood

High Copse

Highwood Copse

Quaves

Burgess Copse

To Upper Basildon
3½ miles

N

Manor Farm

To Bradfield
2 miles

Back La.

START HERE

St Denys Church

Stanford Dingley

Bull P.H.

River Pang

Church
✝ **Bucklebury**

To Hermitage
3¼ miles

Old Boot P.H.

To Southend
1 mile

To Chapel Row
1 mile

0		1 mile
0	1 kilometre	

WALK FOUR:
STANFORD
DINGLEY

$5\frac{1}{2}$ or 6 MILES

The slopes of the Pang Valley provide a typical English patchwork: woods, natural and plantation; fields of grain, grass and pigs; scattered farms, and a village nestling among the trees on the edge of the common.

INTRODUCTION

This walk is about $5\frac{1}{2}$ miles long and should take $3\frac{1}{2}$ hours to do.

Not far from either Reading or the busy M4, Stanford Dingley has managed to escape the attentions of road wideners and house builders. Standing astride the River Pang, it retains a rare tranquillity, its winding street a treasure trove of old buildings. The village name is derived from two of its former inhabitants: William de Stanford, who in 1224 was lord of the manor, and Richard Dyneley, who must surely have been of some local importance, as his other claim to fame, that his father was member of Henry VI's bodyguard, seems a little weak.

There has been a village here since before the Norman Conquest; a mill and ploughlands were mentioned in the Domesday Book. Today the village boasts various seventeenth- and eighteenth-century houses and cottages, including the former smithy adjacent to its minute cottage. This stands opposite The Bull, a seventeenth-century coaching in with a cosy interior featuring a log fire and timber beams.

Although mainly residential now, the village has supported various industries down the ages. The mill mentioned in Domesday has a successor built of brick and weatherboard, and beside it there used to be a tannery. This exploited the plentiful supplies of oak bark stripped from the branches of the oak trees which grow so freely in the vicinity.

Perhaps the most notable building in the village is the charming church of St Denys, which is probably one of the earliest in Berkshire and has existed in one form or another for almost 1,000 years. There was a church here before the Norman Conquest, but the building we see today is largely the result of building which took place around 1200. Notable features of this period are the splendid door with its original ironwork and the wall paintings in the nave, discovered while the church was being restored in 1870. The modern lectern on the north side of the chancel depicts St Denys, to whom the church was dedicated in the thirteenth century. As he was martyred by being beheaded, he is portrayed decapitated, holding his head in his hands.

THE WALK

To commence the walk, turn left, walk 600 metres up the lane, past the crossroads to a stile in the hedgeline on the left. Cross the stile and follow the path across fields up to the woodlands at the top of the slope.

Since leaving the church the walk has been a gradual but continual climb. The countryside through which the walk passes splits roughly into two areas: the high ground towards Frilsham and the lower river valley near Stanford Dingley. The walk started in the base of the Pang valley where the ground is underlain by porous chalk. The higher ground to the north and south of this valley is formed from layers of sand

and clay and of plateau gravels. These produce poor soils which are of little use for agriculture and, like many other similar locations in Berkshire, ended up as commons at Bucklebury and Frilsham or were left as woodland.

Enter the woods and turn left. At the next waymark the path goes uphill and eventually broadens out into a major forest track. Follow this until you meet the road.

Although this area has long been clothed with trees, the composition of the woods we see today is greatly different from what would naturally occur. Much of the old deciduous woodland has been felled in order to allow faster-growing conifers to be planted. Large areas have been dedicated to the mass production of small Norway Spruce trees for the Christmas tree market. However, certain areas do still contain stands of trees native to the area and the fact that woodland has remained on the site, in some cases since at least 1600, has allowed many woodland plants to survive, albeit in the shade of exotic tree species. Ecologists are able to judge the value of such woods for wildlife by measuring the number of woodland indicator species – plants which are closely associated with woodland habitat and rarely found elsewhere. Up to eighteen such species still survive in these woods.

Turn left, and follow the road for 100 metres before turning down a bridleway on the right. Follow this path through the woods until you emerge on a minor road. Turn right and pass through a kissing gate.

The church of St
Denys, Stanford
Dingley

**Follow the path out across the fields to the Pot Kiln
public house.**

The Pot Kiln provides good food at sensible prices
and well-kept real ales. With a garden in which to sit
and enjoy the views of the surrounding woods and
fields in summer, and warm intimate bars for the
colder months, it is an ideal place to rest en route. In
the field opposite is a strange circular depression, a
relic of the brick industry which once flourished in
the area. No doubt many of the cottages in Frilsham
and elsewhere nearby were built of locally produced
brick. Other small pits, for the extraction of either

clay or chalk, can be found scattered throughout the local area. Most are now disused and abandoned and are clogged with vegetation or unfortunately, in some cases, with rubbish.

Walk past the Pot Kiln for 100 metres before crossing a stile on the right-hand side of the lane. Cross the field and walk up into the wood. Walk through the wood for 400 metres until you reach a junction with the forest track walked earlier. Go straight on across the track and follow the woodland path down through Quavies to where it meets a small lane. Walk down the lane.

On your way down the lane you should see several green, red and white posts. These indicate the location of one of the twelve Berkshire County Council Roadside Nature Reserves. These are designated at the request of the local Naturalists' Trust or English Nature and are sites with high wildlife value. The verge has a special management regime tailored to the plant species being conserved, to allow them to flower and set seed before the verge is cut. The plants being protected here are a rich assemblage of woodland flowers, the deep shady lane providing a damp habitat not unlike a woodland. Indeed, this area would once have been woodland, and the hedgerow and verge may represent remnants of the original habitat left after the fields on either side were cleared of trees.

At the bottom of the lane you will reach a road. Turn left and walk along this road for 400 metres before turning right into a narrow deep lane enclosed by

The Bull Inn, at the centre of Stanford Dingley village

high hedges. This lane leads down to the course of the River Pang.

The grass-filled ditch before you is the course of the River Pang. The leaflet first used to promote this walk talked of small trout darting back and forth in the river's clear waters. Today there is no guarantee that there will be any water in the watercourse at all at this point. Although the Pang's upper reaches towards its source near Compton are referred to as a river, in spite of being dry for most of the year, it is really an intermittent chalkland stream. Such streams are often called 'winterbournes' because they only flow after the winter rains. The porous chalk in the valley floor acts as a reservoir, filling up with water during wet weather. When the surface of this reservoir, the water table, reaches ground level in the floor of the valley, then water flows in the river.

Over the centuries there have been periods of drought when the miller at Frilsham Mill had no source of power for months at a time, but recently such dry periods have extended into years. The point from which the river flows all the year round has moved downstream from Frilsham to Stanford Dingley, and even here it is sometimes little more than a trickle. This is partly due to the recent run of dry winters and summer droughts, but undoubtedly the Thames Water pumping station at Compton is also responsible. Here drinking water is pumped up from the same chalk as that which supplies the river's water. Thames Water have now undertaken to reduce abstraction by two thirds, and new sources of supply are being sought.

It remains to be seen which of the two factors affecting the river – abstraction or weather – are most responsible for the low flows. What is clear is that unless some way of returning water to the Pang is found there will continue to be a sad loss of wildlife and attractive scenes in the valley and its villages.

Take the path alongside the watercourse, then follow the waymarks across the meadows to Stanford Dingley.

You will pass through a number of meadows which contain unimproved grassland. These are areas that farmers have not ploughed, nor have they applied fertiliser or herbicides. This has allowed a wide range of grasses and broadleaved herbs to survive. Fields such as these would once have been common along the valley. Although it depends upon the time of year and what amount of grazing there has recently been in the fields, it is worth keeping your eyes open for wild flowers on this part of the walk.

When you reach the road the church of St Denys, the start point for the walk, stands opposite. Turn right if you wish to explore the village.

HOW TO GET THERE

By Car

Located in the maze of minor roads to the west of Reading, Stanford Dingley is not easy to find. Try approaching from the Theale direction, through Bradfield along the Bucklebury road, turning off when you see the appropriate signpost.

By Bus

The Bee Line Bus Company runs a service from Reading to Newbury, service 100/110 via Yattendon which is a short walk to the north of the Pot Kiln public house at Frilsham, an alternative starting point for this walk. Bee Line service 101 between Newbury and Reading via Bradfield Queens Head and Bucklebury Common a short walk to the south of Stanfield Dingley.

REFRESHMENTS

The Pot Kiln public house in Frilsham, and The Bull and The Bat inns at Stanfield Dingley.

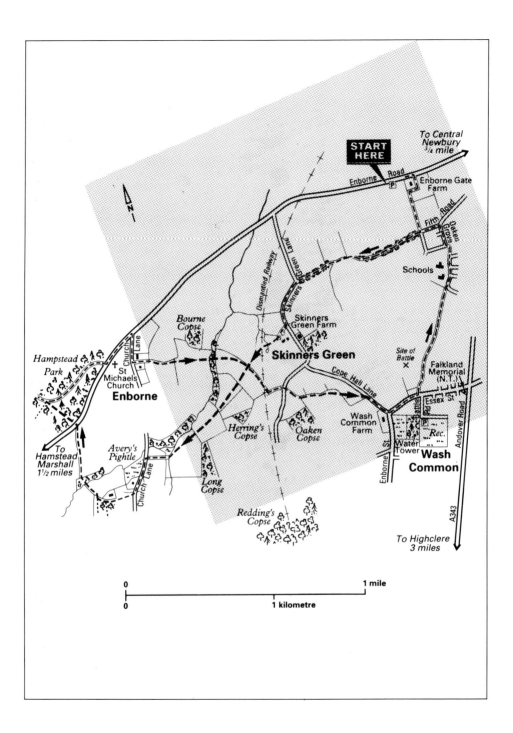

WALK FIVE:
WASH COMMON

2 MILES

A landscape where battle lines were once drawn shows few signs of the conflict today. Even the railway line, so recently abandoned, is rapidly absorbed into the web of hedgerows and copses which span the valley.

INTRODUCTION

The walk is about 2 miles long and should take about
$1\frac{1}{2}$ hours to complete. There is an opportunity to
extend the walk to 4 miles ($2\frac{1}{2}$ hours) by including
the western loop. The route has been described from
the Enborne Road at Enborne Gate Farm, but can
be started from Wash Common, where car parking is
also available. The walk explores an attractive area
which is surprisingly tranquil considering its location
so close to Newbury. However, it was also the scene
of a bloody conflict in the past, and the route takes
you across the battlefield.

THE WALK

**Follow the path through the farm yard. Just past the
house turn right, then left. At the end of the path
(junction of Fifth Road) turn right onto the field path
and the start of the circular walk.**

This path was once the main road into Newbury from
the small hamlet of Skinners Green, and used to be
hedged on both sides. You will see up towards Wash
Common a wooded spur running off the plateau.
This is known locally as Round Hill, an important
site in the first Battle of Newbury.

Follow the path as far as Skinners Green Lane, where you should turn left and follow the road to turn right just before Skinners Green Farm. The path goes past the farm buildings and crosses a meadow towards the old Winchester railway line.

This abandoned railway line is an example of the speed with which nature takes over when man's back is turned. This line was in use until 1962 and the track was not taken up until five years after that. Nonetheless, the embankments are now clothed in thickets of thorn scrub amongst which young sapling trees are gaining a foothold. The ballast on which the rails lay forms a very poor soil, but has rapidly been colonised by many plants now uncommon in the heavily fertilised countryside around about. Derelict railway lines form wonderful green corridors down which wildlife can travel. This section of line resembles an overgrown green lane or double hedgerow and will provide food and shelter for large numbers of woodland birds, mammals and insects. Many of these will have moved up from where the line passes through Redding's Copse just to the south of this walk. Unfortunately, this valuable new wildlife habitat will be lost in the future when the Newbury Bypass, planned to follow the route of the old railway for a distance, is built. Road traffic, competition from which forced this line to close, will dance on the railway's grave.

Cross the embankment and follow the waymarks to the stile in the field to the left. Cross the stile; here a choice can be made.

For the short walk turn left. This route description continues after the section on St Michael's Church.

For the longer walk, from the stile continue straight ahead across the field to a small bridge. From the bridge the path crosses four more fields and ends at a small lane. Turn left and walk up the lane.

On the right is a small nature reserve managed by the Berks., Bucks., and Oxon. Naturalists' Trust, called Avery's Pightle. The reserve is open to the public, although dogs are not allowed when sheep are grazing in late summer and early autumn. The strange word pightle (which rhymes with title) is medieval and describes a small enclosed meadow, which is what the site remains to this day. It has escaped the drainage, ploughing and application of fertilisers and pesticides which have reduced so many other fields in West Berkshire to uninteresting grass monocultures. Indeed, the traces of ridge and furrow cultivation, which are best seen in winter, prove that the site has not been ploughed for centuries.

As a result of this, and because the uneven drainage of the ground produces a variety of soil conditions, this small field is remarkably rich in plants. The damp soils take longer to warm up in summer so the flowers are at their best between the end of June and September, later than you would expect elsewhere. Should you take time to wander around the reserve, please take every care not to damage or disturb the wildlife.

Carry on up Church Lane and turn right at the next footpath. This path runs along a field edge and through some hawthorn bushes to another stile. Cross

Opposite: Following the line of the Parliamentarian advance up Round Hill to Wash Common

71

the stile and walk diagonally left through the gate to another stile. The path then goes uphill to Enborne Road. Cross the road and enter Hamstead Park beside the Park gate.

The word Hamstead derives from an earlier word, 'hamstede', meaing homestead; the nearby settlement of Hamstead Marshall was named after the homestead of the Marshalls because in earlier centuries the manor was held by successive Lord Marshalls of England. In 1176 John, the third Lord Marshall, took Marshall as his family name. First mention of the Park dates from 1229 when the king granted twenty does to William Marshall, and the Park then followed the same descent as the manor. Hamstead Park was named by King Richard III, who used to stay in the lodge and hunt game in the 700 acres. In 1620 the first Earl of Craven was granted ownership of the estate, and in 1626 Sir William Craven, son of the Lord Mayor of London, was created Baron Craven of Hamstead Marshall for services rendered in the Civil War, and in 1662 made an earl. The old manor was pulled down and a new one built in 1665; although this was destroyed in the next century, the walled kitchen gardens are notable survivors. The estate remained in the hands of the Craven family until the death of the seventh earl in 1983. Since then the estate has been sold off in lots to different buyers.

The Park is an entirely man-made landscape designed to conform to an ideal of nature and to provide a huge rural garden for the manor. The

Opposite: One of the entrances to Hamstead Park

original decision for its location may have been guided by the local geology. As at Wash Common

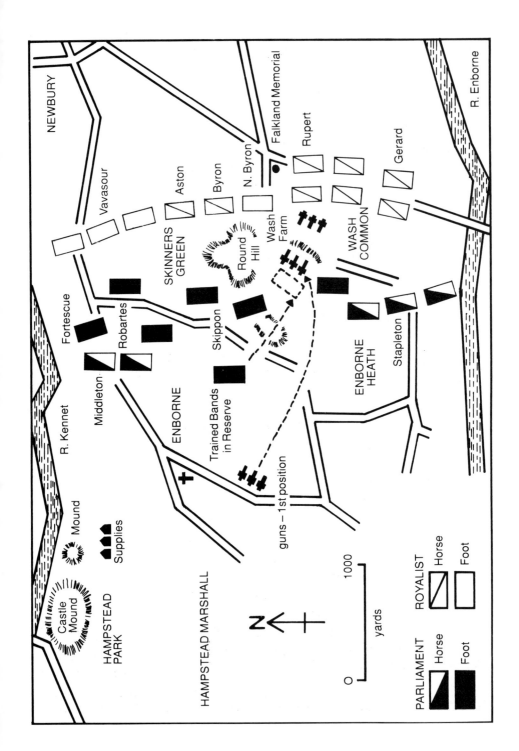

and Greenham Common on the far side of Newbury, the Park occupies an area underlain by sands and gravels which produce poor, dry, acid soils. The Park may therefore have been established on land left over after the more fertile soils in the valleys of the Enborne and Kennet rivers had been brought into cultivation.

Walk up the path which runs between an avenue of lime and beech trees. At the junction with the tarmac drive turn right.

(Should you wish to see more of the Park, do not turn right but carry straight on. This path crosses the Park, passing the site of the manor, before running down to the Kennet and Avon Canal at Hamstead Lock.)

After turning right follow this drive to the large white Park gates on the Enborne Road.

Opposite is the pretty church of St Michael's and All Angels. The age of the church is uncertain, possibly Saxon or early Norman. The font is of Norman origin and is decorated with emblems of the Passion. On the chapel wall is a fourteenth-century fresco painted by an Italian monk from the nearby Sandleford Priory. The bell tower contains one of the oldest bells in England; it was cast in 1260. A colony of brown long-eared bats also inhabit the bell tower. All bats are totally protected under the Wildlife and Countryside Act, 1981.

From the Park gates, turn left down the road. At the

Opposite: Disposition of troops during the Battle of Newbury, 1643

next road junction turn right and follow this road for a short distance. At the footpath sign turn left. Follow this path down into the valley to a small bridge across a ditch.

This is just one of a number of small streams which flow between Enborne and Skinners Green. In the valley, below the sand and gravel beds which form the adjacent higher ground, the land is made up of clay. This does not absorb water, which is obliged instead to run across it, forming these streams. Indeed, the influence of water can be found in local place names; in Wash Common, the wash probably refers to a liability to flood, and Enborne derives from words meaning 'duck stream'.

After crossing the bridge and a field the path goes through a small thorn copse. From the copse walk diagonally left up the meadow to rejoin the shorter walk.

Both walks follow the field edge to the old railway embankment. On top of the bank bear right then left and turn right at the stile on the other side. Turn left onto a gravel drive at the next stile. Follow this drive to the road. Cross the road and walk up the hill to Wash Common.

Lying to the south-west of Newbury, Wash Common and Skinners Green were the scene of one of the bloodiest battles fought during the Civil War (1642–6). On 20 September 1643 the Royalist army under the command of King Charles I met head-on with the Parliamentarian forces of the Earl of Essex. The battle started at first light with a savage artillery duel, followed quickly by cavalry charges led by Prince Rupert (the king's nephew) and Sir John Byron. All day the battle raged, with neither side giving or taking quarter. Some lanes (including Cope Hall Lane to the left of this footpath) were so choked with dead that it was impossible to advance or retreat. In the late afternoon regiments of the London Trained Bands gained a foot-hold on the plateau of the Wash, and slowly pushed the Royalists back. But neither side was in a position to deal a decisive blow.

At the end of the path turn right on to Cope Hall Lane, then left at Essex Street.

Towards evening, the artillery of both sides were firing at point-blank range. The guns of the Parliament were on a line with Wash Common Farm, and the Royalist cannon were 200 yards to the east on Wash Common, roughly where the plantation, the water tower and Battle Road now stand. Sporadic fighting continued into the night. Eventually both sides disengaged and took stock of their situation. Over 6,000 men from both armies had been killed, and many others wounded. Among the dead was the king's secretary Lucius Carey, Lord Falkland. A memorial to him now stands at the junction of Essex Street and the Andover Road. Ammunition, food and water were in very short supply. Essex, knowing his line of march to London was blocked, was committed to another day's fighting. The king, however, informed of the plight of his artillery (they had fired over eighty barrels of powder and didn't have enough for another day of action), decided to retreat

to the Royalist stronghold at Oxford. At dawn, after a brief artillery barrage on the now vacant Royalist positions, Essex found his way to London open. (But find out what happened next, in the Padworth Walk.)

Opposite Wash Common Post Office turn left onto the footpath.

Running along the right-hand side of the path is an unusual natural feature. It is a deep escarpment, which was used as cover to great effect by the Royalist infantry during the battle.

At the end of the path, walk past the John Rankin Infant and Junior Schools, bear left at the playing fields and turn right into Oaken Grove. Turn left at Fifth Road; the end of the walk is now in sight.

HOW TO GET THERE

By Car

Enborne Gate Farm is reached by taking Pound Street from Bartholomew Street in Newbury; follow Pound Street, which then becomes Enborne Road leading to Enborne and Kintbury.

By Bus

Bee Line service N1/N2 bus from Newbury General Post Office to Enborne Road, Kingsbridge Road,

Opposite: Hamstead Park

Elizabeth Avenue, Essex Street (Monday to Saturday). Hampshire Bus service 30/31 from Newbury to Andover serving the Gun public house at Wash Common (Monday to Saturday). Tel. (0256) 464501 for timetable details.

REFRESHMENTS

There are no public houses on the route but they can be found nearby in Wash Common, at Enborne Row and Hamstead Marshall.

Opposite: A Thrift
Wood glade in summer.

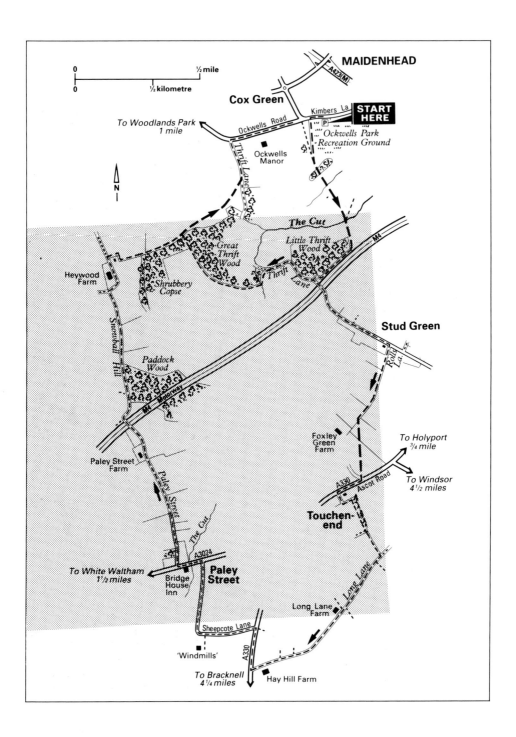

WALK SIX:
COX GREEN

5 MILES

The scattered villages and farmsteads, ancient woods and farm tracks of Cox Green, Touchen-End, and Paley Street have seen sliced through by the M4. Links between local communities of plants and animals as well as of people have been severed and a new sense of separation created.

INTRODUCTION

The walk is about $5\frac{3}{4}$ miles long and should take about 3 hours, but can be shortened to $2\frac{1}{2}$ miles and approximately $1\frac{1}{2}$ hours. It passes through the low-lying agricultural land south of Maidenhead. The route has been described in a clockwise direction from the car park at Ockwells Park, forty-four acres of open parkland managed for recreation by the Royal Borough of Windsor and Maidenhead.

The splendid Ockwells Manor standing beside the recreation ground is an exceptionally interesting example of fifteenth-century domestic architecture. The land on which it stands, once known as Ockholt, was taken into cultivation and then granted to Richard le Norreys in the thirteenth century. The Manor was built by a descendant, Sir John Norreys, between 1446 and 1466, and restored in the twentieth century by Fairfax Wade. The buildings, which are half-timbered with brick filling and are grouped around a small central courtyard, have survived in almost their original state.

The house, plus 250 acres of land, was covenanted to The National Trust in 1945 by Sir John Barry, and although the buildings are not open to the public they can be admired from various points along the walk.

THE WALK

Follow the right-hand park fence towards the woodland strip to join the public footpath. Take this path through the woodland and across the field towards the motorway. The path crosses two bridges, the second of which spans a stream called The Cut. On reaching the motorway embankment, cross the stile and follow the path with the motorway on the left and Little Thrift Wood on the right.

Before the construction of the M4, this area would have been a relatively quiet and secluded part of eastern Berkshire. The A4, which would have taken the east-west traffic, is further to the north in Maidenhead, so apart from the small planes flying from the nearby airfield, there would have been little to disturb the tranquillity of the woods, fields and small villages.

Motorway verges have, however, become important corridors of wildlife habitat. Although busy traffic is alwasy close at hand, the embankments are comparatively free of human interference, and wildlife has been quick to colonise. Kestrels can often be seen hovering in search of small rodents which abound in the long grass. Wildflowers may multiply free from the threat of pesticides and plant collectors, and new species may arrive from further up the road, their seeds carried in the slipstream of passing traffic. In some places road salting can give rise to conditions ideal for the growth of plants more often found near the sea.

Where the motorway cuts through woodland, lines of rhododendrons blossom in June. This plant, a

Crossing The Cut near
Ockwells Park

native of Asia, was introduced into Britain in 1763 as cover for pheasants. It has now become widespread, in some places developing into dense clumps which shade out other plants. There is now growing concern that rhododendrons should sometimes be controlled for the benefit of native plants.

Although the motorway has provided a refuge for some species, for others its presence is a major problem. Every year many animals die trying to cross the motorway, or while scavenging the remains of those which have been killed. Recently more effort has been made to provide tunnels beneath motorways following the lines of previously used animal runs, so that when construction is complete they may continue to patrol their territory in safety.

At the next track junction a choice can be made. For the longer walk, skip forward four paragraphs.

For a shorter walk, turn right along the gravel track called Thrift Lane. At the end of Little Thrift Wood on your right follow the track as it bears left. At the next woodland strip take the footpath on the left. Follow this headland path around the wood, recrossing The Cut. Continue straight ahead towards the next wood, Great Thrift Wood.

The woodland and lane names including the word Thrift preserve a corrupted form of the name of 'the Frith', which once stretched as far as Cruchfield, $2\frac{1}{2}$ miles to the south. It is not clear what 'the Frith' was, although it could have been a large area of woodland, as 'fyrth' was an Anglo-Saxon word for wood and there are many Frith or Frithy Woods elsewhere in the country. Thrift is also an old name for woodland, so these two woods may be the last vestiges of a once much larger forest.

Follow the path around the wood and then through another woodland strip. Turn right after crossing the footbridge to rejoin the longer walk back down to Ockwells Road.

For the longer walk, turn left to cross the motorway bridge. About 250 yards after the track becomes metalled, take the footpath on the right by Rose Cottage, opposite a fishing lake. Walk down this gravel track (Rolls Lane) and at the last house the path leaves the track and veers left along a hedge line to cross a stile into a large field. Follow this field's hedge and turn left through the gate gap in the hedge and cross the stile.

As one walks through this level landscape the wooded Ashley and Bowsey Hills stand out clearly on the north-western skyline. The flat landscape here is typical of the centre of the Thames Valley, and makes it susceptible to flooding. In the past such areas would have been damp and marshy (for example, the place-name of nearby Bray is generally taken to mean 'marsh'), and while higher ground was cultivated, they remained as pasture. Modern-day drainage has helped to dry out the land and allowed its rich alluvial soils to be brought into production. Some fields are now used for high-value market garden crops. However, ridding the land of unwanted water pushes more into the major watercourses, increasing the risk that they will flood. Indeed large areas of countryside (and towns) adjacent to the Thames have been flooded in recent years, and the National Rivers Authority has plans to build a new channel between Maidenhead and Windsor to carry future flood-waters. The proposed channel will be a massive engineering project; it will be like digging out a new River Thames, only with the added problem of needing to go under the M4 and a railway line.

The path then crosses, diagonally right, two fields, to end at a road.

On the right-hand side of the first field stands Foxley Green Farm with its moat. The moat, which survives in good condition, is a scheduled Ancient Monument and like other moated sites in the area is of medieval origin. It is a roughly square-shaped water-filled ditch, which is mostly obscured by the trees growing around it. Moats are strange features of the countryside, very common in some areas such as East Anglia, while almost absent from others, for example Devon and Cornwall. This hints at a fashionable rather than functional reason for their construction.

In 1321 John le Foxley was granted a licence by the Crown to make a park in a clearing in the Royal Forest of Windsor which once extended over this area. The moat excavated around the manor house was ostensibly to help keep out intruders, but the defensive capabilities of such small moats must have been minimal. In reality the motivation behind moat construction was probably to provide a status symbol, a fashion which caught on in some parts of the country more than others. A more practical use of the moat may have been to provide fish and fowl for the manor's table. The manor house burned down in the eighteenth century, after which the land within the moat was used as an orchard.

In this area also look out for the Gurten herd of pedigree Charolais cattle, from small calves through the age range to the massive adults. These white cattle from France were among the first to be introduced into this country to improve our stocks.

This is Touchen-End. Cross the Ascot Road and turn shortly left down the farm track.

The village name of Touchen-End, although sounding vaguely French, is probably derived from two old English words, *twa* (two) and *chene* (chain), and refers to two chains placed across the diverging roads in the village centre, one leading to Hawthorne Hill and the other to White Waltham.

Follow the farm track through this market garden area. At the next track (Long Lane) turn right.

Long Lane is an ancient green lane now classified as a bridleway. The first part of the lane is made up and used by agricultural vehicles to gain access to the fields. Further south-west along the track the lane reverts to a more natural state. The ditches which run along either side of the lane have been neglected and have filled with vegetation. Along parts of the lane they no longer serve their purpose of taking rainwater away from the surface of the land and discharging it elsewhere. Instead, patches of permanently damp soil and ponds have developed and with them characteristic vegetation made up of plant species which thrive in wet ground. Ironically this lane, which may be several centuries old and would once have been better drained than the surrounding land, is now the refuge of those plants and animals driven from nearby fields by drainage. As well as being an attractive right of way the lane is now an important wildlife habitat, so management needs to take into account the needs of the resident plants and animals as well as of walkers and riders. This means that after rain parts of the track can become quite wet, and care may need to be taken to negotiate the waterlogged patches.

Follow Long Lane to the road. Turn right along the road for forty yards, then left into Sheepcote Lane. Follow this lane back around to the main road. Turn left and cross the bridge over The Cut. Next door is the Bridge House Inn, which is open all day and serves refreshments.

The shady path
running beside Little
Thrift Wood

The Cut: a waterway named thus is usually man-made and used for navigation or water supply. Formerly known as the Forest Stream, The Cut was given its present name when a final man-made link was created to provide a continuous watercourse the thirteen miles from Winkfield to the Thames at Bray. The Cut forms an attractive natural corridor across the farmland of the area and is fed by various streams, including one rising from the springs in Great Thrift Wood.

Turn right down the lane (Paley Street), passing some pretty cottages. The lane reverts to a farm track crossing back over the motorway.

Overhead you may see light aircraft. These fly from

the small airfield at White Waltham. This was opened in 1928 as a private landing strip for the owner of Shottesbrooke Park Estate. It was taken over by the government during the war and did not revert into private hands until the early 1980s. There were once twenty-three airfields in Berkshire, but now there are only two: White Waltham, and the military airfield at Greenham Common near Newbury. White Waltham's grass-covered runway is now mainly used for club and recreation flying.

Continue along this track (Snowball Hill), pass through Heywood Farm, and after the white cottage turn right along the headland path. Pass through the hedge (by the electricity pylon) and over the small footbridge to follow the second field's headland path. This path passes Great Thrift Wood. Turn left on to Thrift Lane to rejoin Ockwells Road.

Great Thrift Wood, an ancient woodland, has a good mixture of large and small trees and a rich shrub and ground flora, which indicates a long period of woodland cover. Much of the wood is on level ground and some parts are permanently waterlogged, favouring trees such as willows and alders. There are no conifers and as there has been no recent replanting the native species are distributed naturally through the wood according to their individual soil, water and light requirements. This makes it a valuable wildlife site, as the complex animal and plant communities which have evolved over the centuries and adapted to changing local conditions would be extremely difficult to replace. A plantation woodland, even using the same combination of tree and shrub species, would take centuries to begin to resemble Great Thrift Wood.

Turn right along the road past Ockwells Manor to the Park entrance and the end of the walk.

HOW TO GET THERE

By Car

Take the Cox Green and White Waltham turning off the northbound A423(M) on the south side of Maidenhead. Turn right, then left at the roundabout, and follow signs to Ockwells Park Recreation Ground.

By Bus

The Bee Line Bus Company service No. 55/56 Town Service from Maidenhead to Woodlands Park stops at Cox Green Road, only a short walk from the start of the walk at the Ockwells Park.

REFRESHMENTS

The Bridge House Inn at Paley Street.

TOILETS

At Ockwells Park Recreation Ground car park.

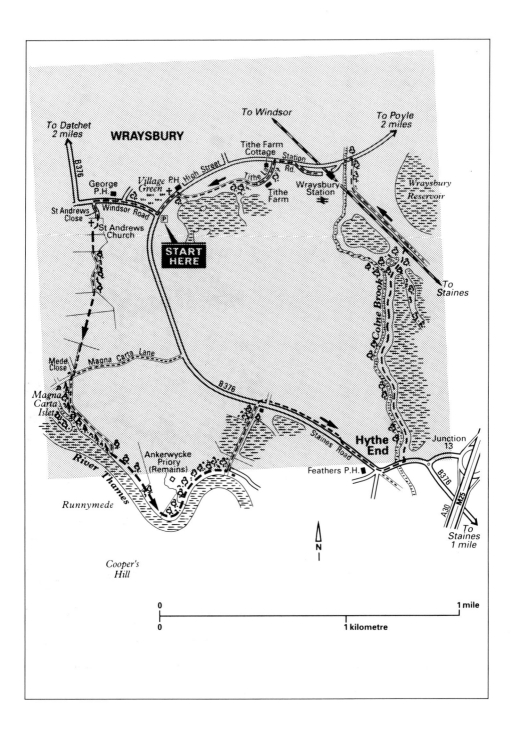

94

WALK SEVEN:
WRAYSBURY

4 MILES

Wraysbury village, hemmed in by reservoirs and lakes formed from flooded gravel pits to the east and the River Thames to the west, has virtually become an island.

INTRODUCTION

It is only natural that a parish which occupies a low-lying area of land between the Thames and one of its tributaries should have a history intimately tied to water. This walk takes you through a part of the Colne Valley Regional Park and leads you alongside the Thames and through the waterland of lakes recently created from flooded gravel pits. The walk is approximately $4\frac{1}{2}$ miles in length and should take 2 hours to complete at a leisurely pace. The route is described in an anti-clockwise direction, starting from the car park opposite Windsor Road in Wraysbury village centre.

THE WALK

From the car park, cross Wraysbury High Street on to Windsor Road. Follow this road past the village green and the George Inn to St Andrew's Close on the left.

Wraysbury village lies in one of the most eastern parts of Berkshire and, located next to the Thames and close to the ancient Crown lands of Windsor, it is of greater historic interest than may appear at first sight. In common with many other places in the flood-plain

Beside the Thames in
the Ankerwycke
Estate

of the River Thames, there are records of Mesolithic
and Neolithic remains as well as those of the Saxon
and Norman periods. The village is mentioned in the
Domesday Book under the name of 'Wyrardusbury',
and is located at the centre of the parish.

Although it must have been a disadvantage to be
located in an area subject to flooding, the rich

alluvial soils resulting from centuries of floods, the close proximity to the river traffic on the Thames, and the source of power the river provided brought Wraysbury people compensations. The problems of flooding were in part addressed by raising roads above flood level; in places it is still possible to see how the roads stand up above the surrounding land.

Wraysbury has a number of inns but The George, which dates back to 1666, is the oldest. There are a number of other seventeenth-century buildings in the village to look out for.

Walk down to the end of the Close and go through the church gate.

It is not known when the first church was built on the site of St Andrew's, although it was probably in Saxon times. The present church dates from the early thirteenth century and was extended in the fifteenth century. It was restored in 1862, when the tower was added. Inside is a large brass depicting a knight in Tudor armour.

Follow the path around the left of the church to its rear. Take the narrow grassed path to the metal kissing gate, pass through this and cross the field to the stile immediately opposite. Follow this footpath across the fields, crossing a number of stiles on the way, until you reach Mede Close.

The damp low-lying nature of the land here is obvious. Although the ditch beside the path may dry up during time of drought, the lines of moisture-loving willows growing along its length show that the water table is never far below the surface.

Turn left and then immediately right into Magna Carta Lane. Turn left over a stile onto the footpath opposite the second house on the right. Follow the footpath until it reaches the edge of the River Thames.

You are walking through a landscape rich in historical incident. Although the story of the Magna Carta – how, in 1215, King John was forced by his barons to seal the document which came to be seen as greatly important in defining the English Constitution – is well known, the actual location of the event has been the subject of considerable speculation. As you follow this path, through the trees on your right you may glimpse Magna Carta Island. Further along is Magna Carta Islet, formerly separated from the bank by part of the river but now connected to the mainland. In the private grounds of Magna Carta House on Magna Carta Island is a stone tablet which was found in the Thames in Victorian times. This may be the table upon which the signing took place, but the Islet has claims to being its original location.

At the riverside, turn left over a stile and continue to follow the path alongside the river until the path ends at a gate.

From this path there are good views across the river to the wooded slopes of Cooper's Hill and the white RAF memorial which names 20,000 airmen who died during the Second World War but who have no known grave. Below the hill are the Runnymede meadows owned by The National Trust. Runnymede is an Anglo-Saxon name meaning 'Council Meadow', and this is another possible Magna Carta signing site. It is certainly the one most well known.

This path leads you through the Ankerwycke Estate, owned by Berkshire County Council. The estate retains the name of the house which was built here in the nineteenth century but has now been demolished. On your left, set back from the river against some woods, are the remains of Ankerwycke Priory. These two double-storey chalk rubble walls are all that is left of the house of Benedictine nuns built in the thirteenth century and dedicated to St Mary Magdalene. The Priory was founded during the reign of Henry II, probably not much before 1160, by the Lord of Wraysbury, Gilbert de Mountfichet. The Priory owned all the weirs and fisheries on the nearby stretch of the Thames between Ankerwycke Ferry and Old Windsor upstream. There are also the remains of two fishponds in the woods behind the ruin. At the beginning of the sixteenth century there were six or seven nuns and a prioress, but by 1536 the Priory had been dissolved.

Near the ruins stands a massive, ancient yew tree, said to be the oldest in Berkshire. Under this tree Henry VIII is reputed to have courted Anne Boleyn. This is another place claimed as the site where Magna Carta was signed. This theory is supported by the ancient ditches which surround the area where the yew tree and the Priory stand. If, in the past, these ditches were filled with river water from the

Thames, then the area would effectively have been an island, essential for any serious claimant.

The last stretch of path along the riverside before the gate takes you through a piece of woodland particularly rich in wildlife because of its combination of wet and dry ground, its proximity to the river, and the mixture of native and introduced tree species.

At the gate turn left and follow the narrow track up to the Staines Road.

The open parkland of the Ankerwycke Estate features many splendid large free-grown trees: oaks, planes and limes. High up in the branches of many of the limes are tangled clumps of mistletoe, which seems to be particularly common in this area. Another unusual feature of the estate is the resident population of ring-necked parakeets. These gaudily coloured birds will be heard and often seen among the parkland trees of the estate. Their calls remind one of zoos or wildlife programmes about exotic places – rather out of place close to the M25 and Heathrow airport. They are the descendants of imported birds which escaped and have naturalised themselves into our countryside and weather.

Using extreme caution, cross to the other side of the Staines Road. Turn right and follow the verge, but after 500 metres, cross the road again (when it is safe to do so) to the footway on the opposite side of the road. Follow this road around to the left to Hythe End Bridge, where you should cross back to the western side of the road. Immediately after crossing the bridge over the Colne Brook River, turn left to follow

a footpath which runs between the river and a flooded gravel pit.

Here in the Thames Valley much of the land is underlain by rich reserves of gravel. This has been dug out on an ever-increasing scale for centuries. The lakes by which you walk on this route are the results of flooding pits after the gravel has been extracted. The complex of lakes at Wraysbury has become important for recreation and for wildlife conservation. Today these lakes provide water-space for sailing and angling clubs, as well as attractive waterside walks. The flood-prone land and water-courses nearby provides sites from which wildlife can rapidly colonise the new lakes. Wildfowl soon found that the irregularly sided lakes with their scattered islands offered shelter from winds and seclusion for breeding, while the varied depth of the lakes provided feeding for a wide range of species. The activity of the nearby airport seems to have little effect on the birdlife of the Wraysbury area, which has something of interest all the year round. In winter diving ducks congregate in large numbers; in summer grebes breed on the lakes and migrant songbirds frequent waterside trees and scrub.

At the end of the gravel pit carry straight on to the railway. Taking particular care, cross over the railway, turn left and follow the path to where it brings you out onto Coppermill Road.

Coppermill Road is a reminder of important water-powered industries from Wraysbury's past. Two mills in Wraysbury were mentioned in the Domesday

Opposite: The River Thames at Runny-mede

Book. During the eighteenth century there were important paper mills at Wraysbury and at nearby Horton, the former having been in operation since 1605. Perhaps influenced by market changes, in 1772 Wraysbury Mill, here on the Colne Brook, changed to working as an iron mill, and five years later to a copper mill. The copper ore was brought up the Thames by barge and then carried to the mill by horse. The other Wraysbury Mill stood near the junction of the Colne Brook and the Thames at Hythe End.

Cross over the Colne Brook, pass Wraysbury Station and continue along Station Road. Just before you reach Tithe Farm Cottage, turn left and walk down Tithe Lane and onto a footpath called 'The Worple'. This finally opens out onto the edge of Wraysbury Lakes. Follow the footpath until you reach Wraysbury High Street. Turn left and walk along the High Street to the start of the walk.

HOW TO GET THERE

By Car

Wraysbury village is approached by following the B376 from Datchet in the west or from Junction 13 on the M25 in the east, the latter perhaps being the less complicated route. There is car parking in the village opposite Windsor Road or to the rear of the village green, as well as at Wraysbury Station.

By Bus

Ashford Luxury Coaches service 305 between Staines, Colnebrook and Poyle stops at Wraysbury Station (Monday to Friday, once per day, Saturday four times per day). Tel. 081 890 6394 for timetable details. Nightingale Coaches service 560 runs between Slough, Datchet, Horton and Wraysbury Station (Monday to Saturday – hourly service). Tel. (0753) 887294 for timetable details.

By Train

British Rail operate a regular service between Windsor and Staines stopping at Wraysbury Station which is passed on the walk. Tel. (0734) 595911 for information.

REFRESHMENTS AND FACILITIES

Available at the three pubs passed on the walk. There is a general store in Hythe End and a range of shops, and a post office in Wraysbury.

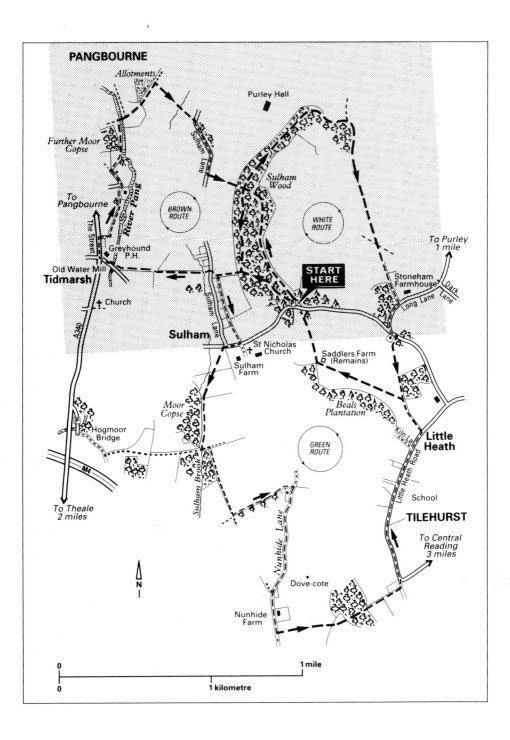

PANGBOURNE

Allotments

Purley Hall

Further Moor
Copse

Sulham Lane

Sulham Wood

To
Pangbourne

River Pang

The Street

BROWN
ROUTE

WHITE
ROUTE

To Purley
1 mile

Greyhound
P.H.

START
HERE

Stoneham
Farmhouse

Dark Lane

Old Water Mill

Long Lane

Tidmarsh

+ Church

Sulham Lane

Sulham

St Nicholas
Church

Saddlers Farm
(Remains)

A340

Sulham
Farm

Moor
Copse

Beals
Plantation

Kiln Lane

Little
Heath

Hogmoor
Bridge

GREEN
ROUTE

Little Heath Road

M4

School

To Theale
2 miles

Sulham Brook

TILEHURST

Nunhide Lane

To Central
Reading
3 miles

N

Dove-cote

Nunhide
Farm

0   1 mile

0   1 kilometre

WALK EIGHT:
SULHAM VALLEY   3 MILES

The small hay fields and pastures of the damp valley bottom (on the left) contrast with the large grain fields of the free-draining slopes and hilltop (to the right). The shape of Sulham Woods clearly follows the line of the valley side.

INTRODUCTION

The Sulham Valley walks consist of three circular routes which are $2\frac{1}{2}$ miles (Brown route), 3 miles (White route), and $4\frac{1}{2}$ miles (Green route) in length, and will take 1, $1\frac{1}{2}$, and $2\frac{1}{2}$ hours respectively to walk. They have been described from the Forestry Commission's car park at Sulham Wood. Car parking is also available at Pangbourne, Theale, Little Heath and Hogmoor Bridge, from where one or other of these walks can be started. Each walk has the appropriate colour background on its waymarks – Brown, White or Green – and the waymarks carry the words 'Recreational Route'. A section of the Brown and White routes use a 'Permitted Path'.

The Sulham Valley is unspoiled, but it is close to the built-up areas of Tilehurst, Pangbourne, Purley and Theale. The valley is unusual because two streams – the Pang and the Sulham Brook – run through it, side by side. There are woods on the lower ground among traditionally farmed small fields, creating a patchwork rich in nature conservation interest. Public footpaths offer several pleasant walks through the area.

BROWN ROUTE

The Brown route, approximately $2\frac{1}{2}$ miles long, runs through the meadows by the River Pang. Waterproof shoes are recommended; the walk should take about 1 hour.

Follow the Brown background waymarks down through the wood to the edge of a field where the circular walk begins. Cross the stile, follow the path to the road, and cross it to take the waymarked path nearly opposite.

The path crosses the tiny Sulham Brook, then runs through some small fields. The ground here is frequently wet, as can be seen from the numerous moisture-loving trees such as alders and willows which abound in the hedgerows and nearby woodlands.

As you walk through these fields you will see a number of squat concrete buildings half hidden in the hedgerows. These are pill-boxes which were built in 1940 during the Second World War. At that time, military strategists considered that a route to the west of London was the one most likely to be taken by Hitler's troops during an invasion. The pill-boxes in the Sulham Valley formed part of a line of defence which ran from south of Reading, along the Kennet and Avon Canal, up the Sulham Valley and along the Thames. There was also an anti-tank ditch which linked the Thames to the canal, both uncrossable by tanks, which although now filled in is still visible in places on this walk. Later on this walk you may see a partly destroyed box which was used by British artillery for practice in destroying German pill-boxes in the run up to D-Day.

After crossing the River Pang turn right at the road.

Opposite is the Old Water Mill. There has been a mill in Tidmarsh since at least 1239 for grinding corn or fulling cloth. In the 1920s the present mill was the home of the author Lytton Strachey, a member of a group of artists and intellectuals which included Virginia Woolf.

Walk down to the next road junction.

A detour to the left leads to Tidmarsh Church. It has a Norman doorway but most of the structure dates from the thirteenth century. As well as carved oak beams, other unusual features can be seen. The apse (arched recess) is of a unique design, being octagonal in shape with small stained-glass windows set in each face. During the nineteenth century, several wall paintings were discovered in the apse. The restorer, lacking today's skills, picked out each of the figures in purple paint! The sculptured Norman font was found buried in the churchyard a century ago.

Turn right along the main road (past the Greyhound public house) and walk through the village of Tidmarsh.

You are walking along the Pangbourne to Theale road, here known as The Street. This route through Tidmarsh has always been busier than the parallel

Strolling down into the valley from Sulham Woods

route through Sulham, much of which is now little more than a track. The Tidmarsh road was a turnpike; look out for the charming octagonal toll cottage which stands on the right-hand side of the road.

At a field entrance turn right off the main road. Pass through the kissing gate and follow the route through several waymarked turns, to the River Pang.

Here, in its lower reaches, the Pang is a typical chalk stream, fast, clear, and ideal for trout. At its water's edge varieties of rush and reed grow alongside other plants such as water mint and marsh marigold.

Follow the path along the riverbank until it crosses a footbridge (at this point the link path from Pangbourne joins the route). The path crosses the valley bottom with one sharp right turn halfway across the

open meadows. **On reaching Sulham Lane, turn right, and follow the road before taking the path on the left which goes uphill into Sulham Wood. A few yards into the wood turn right and follow the waymarks along the woodland edge back to the car park.**

WHITE ROUTE

Follow the White background waymarks through the Forestry Commission's Sulham Woods.

Although these woodlands are extremely popular with local people for walking, their prime purpose is to produce timber for poles or pulping. The tree species selected are those which are best suited to the soil conditions, and on this section of the walk they include large stands of conifers: Norway spruce, Douglas fir and Scots pine. These trees cast a dense shade so in places few plants grow beneath them, but along the paths and rides where light still penetrates or where the natural tree species have been allowed to remain, there are still carpets of wild flowers. The bluebells are a great attraction in spring.

Continue through a beech wood along the hillside.

Beech trees are often associated with thin dry chalk soils as are found here. Although it is unlikely any tree would relish these conditions, beech trees seem able to survive once established and old specimens can grow to a considerable size, although, as these woods show, they are often vulnerable to storm damage. Beech nuts – mast – provide food for animals, while the leaf litter and fallen branches on the ground, as well as the trees themselves, are host to many kinds of fungus.

This path offers views of Purley Hall. The name Purley is derived from the word 'porlei' meaning ' a clearing in the woods for snipe and bittern'. These are both marsh birds, and this early name hints at the wet conditions found in the valley in former times. Purley Hall, previously known as Hyde Hall, was built by Francis Hyde in 1609. Anne Hyde married James II and was mother to Queen Mary and Queen Anne. During the eighteenth century many specimen and parkland trees were planted in the grounds of the house, and ornamental canals excavated.

The (permitted) path continues around the edge of the wood, then uphill between large fields.

From the edge of the wood you will have spectacular views of the Thames Valley stretching away towards Goring Gap to the north-west. Rising on either side of the valley are the wooded chalk hills of the Chilterns on the right and the edge of the Berkshire Downs on the left. The valley has been cut down through the chalk by thousands of years of river erosion. The Goring Gap is one of only a few places where a river has cut its way through the western escarpment of the chalk uplands which stretch from south-west to north-east across southern England, and it is certainly the most spectacular. It has become an important transport route avoiding high ground.

Follow the hedge downhill between Stoneham Farm and another wood to reach Long Lane. At the road

junction turn right (take care to walk on the right to be seen by cars). Cross the stile opposite the next road junction. This path runs downhill between open fields, and crosses a shallow dip by another wood. Here the route takes a sharp right turn. (From here the path coincides with Green route back to the car park.) The path crosses open fields and passes the remains of Sadler's Farm and a large pond. Follow the waymarks to the right, and the starting point will be in view.

GREEN ROUTE

From the car park follow the track down through the Forestry Commission woods, then across a field (this coincides with the Brown route). Before the bottom of the field is reached turn left to run along the rear of some gardens until the road between Tilehurst and Tidmarsh is reached.

Opposite stands Sulham Church. The original thirteenth-century church built on this site was pulled down in 1832 and replaced by the present church in 1838. It was built by the Revd John Wilder, Rector for fifty-six years and a member of a family which was the main landowner in the Sulham area for three hundred years. The marble font dates from 1733 and was presumably rescued from the earlier church. The design for the present church is the result of twin influences: a visit the Revd Wilder had made to Italy; and the interest at the time in the study and imitation of churches of the Middle Ages. It is built of flint and stone and the tall spire contains brilliantly-coloured lancet windows. John Wilder also built several of the pretty, Romantic-style thatched cottages in the village, as well as the village school, now closed.

Turn right down the road for a few yards, then left into a field. Follow the path across the fields towards the woods.

These low-lying, seasonally wet fields are unsuited to cultivation using modern machinery and are still either grazed by cattle and horses or cut for hay as they have been for many years. The scenery here has probably changed little in decades.

The path runs along the edge of Moor Copse on your right. At this point the waymarked link-path from the Hogmoor Bridge comes in from the west.

The vast majority of the numerous woodlands found up and down the Sulham Valley are part of a large Site of Special Scientific Interest. The woods all have individual names which hint at their long history and use: Moor Copse, Oxley's Copse, Herridge's Copse and Peatpits Wood. Some of the woods are still actively coppiced and this helps to conserve the rich flora and fauna which inhabit them. Variations in the topography, soils and drainage of the valley bottom as a whole have created a mosaic where vegetation and associated wildlife can change over very short distances. A copse beside a river with saturated peaty soils may lie in close proximity to the ridges and hummocks of a slightly higher pasture where gravelly, free-draining soils encourage an entirely different mix of plants.

Agricultural intensification has drained most wet areas of southern England. The Sulham Valley, retaining this rich collection of traditionally managed woodland and pasture, is an important nature conservation area. Another result of the conservation of these habitats is that they add greatly to the beauty of the landscape, which is here designated part of an Area of Outstanding Natural Beauty.

After two changes of direction, the route leaves the woodland to run between fields. At the junction of footpaths turn left to Nunhide Lane. Turn right down the lane to Nunhide Farm, then left after passing by the farm, and up a slope towards the woods.

On the slope to the rear of the farm is a brick tower. This may have been designed as a dovecote – a building used for breeding pigeons for the table – or simply as a folly. It was built by John Wilder and is sometimes known as Wilder's Folly.

Walk up through the woods. Skirt the playing-field beyond to reach the road. Turn left along Little Heath Road and follow it along the edge of Tilehurst. After nearly a mile, just past Kiln Lane, the walks turn off to the left. This leads over the fields past the remains of Sadler's Farm, and coincides with the White route to the end of the walk.

HOW TO GET THERE

By Car

The car park at Sulham Woods is reached along the Tidmarsh to Tilehurst road west of Reading.

By Bus

The Bee Line Bus Company service 5 between Reading and Oxford, and service 100 and 110 between Reading and Newbury both stop at Pangbourne. Services 101/102/103 between Reading and Newbury stop in Theale. Reading Transport Company services 38 and 39 run from Reading Station to Little Heath. Reading Buses service 33 runs between Reading railway station and Bitterne Avenue. Turnham House on the Green route is only a short walk from this last stop.

By Train

British Rail run services to Theale and Pangbourne Stations. For timetable information Tel. Reading 595911 or Newbury 40656.

REFRESHMENTS

The Greyhound Inn at Tidmarsh.

TELEPHONE

There are public payphones in Tidmarsh and on the roadside near Sulham Church.

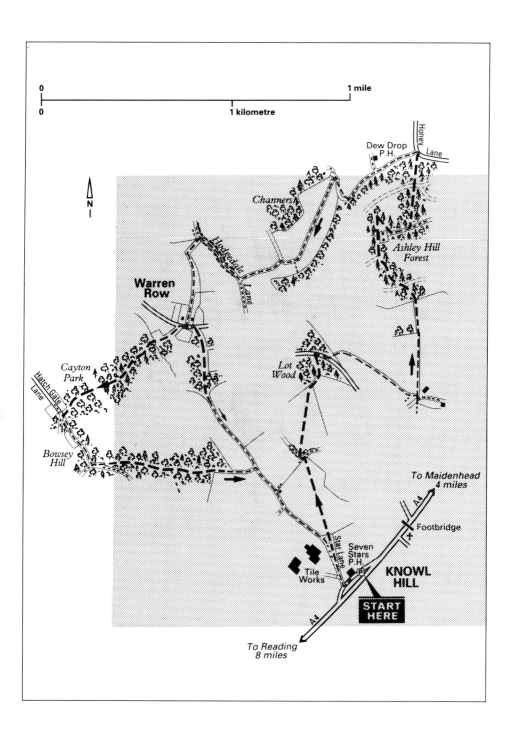

WALK NINE:
KNOWL HILL

4 MILES

There is a clear difference between the conifer plantations on Ashley Hill (top right) and the natural woodland of Cayton Park (bottom left). The clay quarry for the tile works is visible cutting into the woods in the bottom left.

INTRODUCTION

This walk is approximately $4\frac{1}{2}$ miles long and should take about 3 hours to complete, although by taking the short-cut the length can be shortened to $3\frac{1}{2}$ miles. The walk explores an intimate, undulating wooded landscape to the north-east of Twyford, and is described in an anti-clockwise direction from the lay-by at the Seven Stars public house, Knowl Hill.

The wooded height of Ashley Hill is a notable landmark across a wide area of eastern Berkshire. The tall conifers on its summit lend it extra height, so that it stands out above the surrounding Thames Valley landscape. The hill and the surrounding area are an attractive mix of woodlands, pasture, and small villages, identified as an Area of Special Landscape Importance.

The existence of Ashley Hill, like that of the slightly lower Bowsey Hill to the west, is due to the land surface's underlying geology. The rocks and clays below the ground have given the landscape its shape and have influenced the way in which the land has been employed and settled over the years. The same can of course be said of most parts of the countryside, but the geology here is particularly interesting and so will be explained in a little more detail.

The less permeable clays which predominate in this area made it less attractive for agriculture than the reasonably fertile but better-drained soils nearby. The prevalence of springs which saturate parts of the land at certain times of the year also made anything but pasture a headache, and much of the land remained under woodland. The same remains true today, but last century the natural beauty of the area was noticed and a number of large houses situated in extensive grounds were built, hidden among the woods. Although close to the busy A4 and not far from Reading, the area still remains peaceful.

THE WALK

Set off up Star Lane, passing the tile factory on your left.

There are significant outcrops of impermeable London Clay suitable for use in brick and tile making under Ashley and Bowsey Hills. Today the Knowl Hill works, which has been established here for 160 years, is the only remaining traditional clay tile manufacturer left in Berkshire. The clay is extracted from the side of Bowsey Hill to the north of the works and stockpiled in the open. It is then allowed to weather for two years, being turned over regularly during the process. The clay is then squeezed many times to remove lumps and air pockets before being shaped into tiles, or into more elaborate designs, such as gryphons and dragons, for ridge-tile ornaments. These are then dried in large heated rooms before being put into the kiln to be fired. The tiles must be thoroughly dried and completely free from

water, or they will crack in the kiln. Some of the more detailed designs are still dried naturally in the rooms above the kiln, as all the tiles were in the past.

Where the lane bears around to the left, cross the stile straight ahead and follow the cross-field path up the hill. The route meets several other paths and tracks by a house. Follow the waymarkers around to the left of the house and take the path at its rear diagonally across the field.

As you walk up the slope you will see in front of you a fine view of Ashley Hill. Ashley Hill is made up of three geological layers: Reading Beds at the bottom, then London Clay, finally capped with glacial sand and gravel. The Reading Beds here are approximately 56 feet thick, and consist of clays and sands, sediments which were laid down by rivers draining eastwards around fifty million years ago. Fossils of oysters and fish teeth have been found in these beds, along with the remains of various plants. The remainder of the beds consist of multi-coloured silts and clays with some lenses of sand deposited by occasional stronger water currents.

At the far side of the field cross two stiles to enter Lot Wood. The path emerges from the wood onto a minor road. Turn right and walk along the road for about 50 yards before turning left onto a concrete track. Shortly afterwards, turn right by the cattle pens onto a path which runs alongside a field fence down to the next path junction by a stile. Here turn left and walk up the fields alongside the hedgerow, crossing two stiles as you go, towards Ashley Hill Forest on the skyline.

Opposite: In Lot Wood

123

Ashley Hill Forest and Lot Wood are leased and managed by the Forestry Commission. On Ashley Hill a large number of paths and woodland rides are available for public use, making it an ideal place for walks. The wide tracks are built into the forest to make it easier to carry out forestry operations. They also make ideal all-weather walking routes and provide circuits of the forest.

These woods are interesting because of the way that the woodland is managed, the different species of trees planted, and the plants, birds, animals, and fungus which can be found here throughout the year. Since this is a managed woodland, from time to time forestry work will be carried out. This may be routine thinning, where slow-growing trees are removed to allow those remaining to grow on more strongly, or clear-felling, where whole swathes of woodland are felled and the timber removed before planting with new trees. This activity can have a dramatic impact on the peace and tranquillity of the wood, but without long-term management woodlands such as this would produce little valuable timber. If forestry operations are in progress, take care to keep a safe distance away.

Cross the stile into the wood and follow the path up the hill to where the old Keeper's Cottage stood. Follow the track alongside the boundary fence of Keeper's Cottage to the next track junction where you should turn right back on yourself to walk up to the main drive to the house.

If you look around the hilltop you will see the stumps of trees which have recently been thinned. Some of

Star Lane running up the slope of Bowsey Hill

the stumps have been partly pulled out of the ground, and it is possible to see the poor pebbly soils in which the trees are growing.

Glacial sand and gravel occurs on this hilltop, as it does on much of the higher ground above the

125

Thames Valley. The pebbles and sand-grains of flint, chert, and quartz are of many sizes. Some pebbles are flint fossils of sea urchins, belemnites (finger-shaped cases of squid-like creatures), and sponges. The gravels were deposited over 100,000 years ago when ice sheets extended into southern England during a period of glaciation. The gravels may have been deposited from rivers of meltwater gushing from the edge of the ice-sheet, or perhaps by the River Thames when its level was far higher than it is today.

At the main gate to the house, turn left down the drive and then shortly afterwards turn left down the next path. This leads downhill to Honey Lane.

Notice that you walk through an even-aged stand of beech trees. These hardwood trees will take longer to mature than the quick-growing conifers, but may eventually be more valuable. The woodland floor is heavily shaded in summer and so supports few plants, but in spring is thick with bluebells.

On reaching the lane, turn left and walk along a surfaced track, passing the Dew Drop Inn public house on your right. Follow the track through the five-bar gate and at the next path junction turn right down a narrow path. Shortly after passing a cottage on your right, cross the stile on the left. Follow the path across the field to a gravel track. You will see brick buildings among the trees of Cayton Park in the distance: this is the village of Warren Row.

Looking to your right you will see gently rolling fields, a landscape typical of chalk geology. This area

Shade and shelter in
one of Bowsey Hill's
many green lanes

is the southern fringe of a major belt of chalk uplands
which make up the Chiltern Hills. These can be seen
in the distance to the north in Buckinghamshire on
the far side of the River Thames.

**Follow the track down the slope to where it turns
sharply left. Take the path to the right (a bridleway
named Hodgedale Lane) and after about 400 yards
cross the stile on the left before following the path up
to the road at Warren Row.**

127

Here a choice can be made.

For the shorter walk turn left and then almost immediately right onto a track. Follow this track to a stile, cross this, and then follow the path down to Star Lane. Continue down the lane to the end of the walk.

For the longer walk turn right along the road for a short distance before turning left onto a footpath. This path leads up through the woods of Cayton Park, at one point crossing a wide ride. The path ends on Hatch Gate Lane at Bowsey Hill.

This park is a good example of ancient woodland, with over a hundred species of wild plants identified. Ancient woodlands are those which are known to have had continuous tree cover since at least AD 1600. They are therefore representative of the 'wildwood' which used to cover the whole of the British Isles. However, they are only semi-natural because they have been altered and managed by man since at least Roman times. Ancient woodlands are important as wildlife habitats for a number of reasons. Those plants and animals originally resident in the wildwood will have had the chance to survive in uninterrupted woodland conditions. These species may be very slow to colonise newly planted woodlands, and hence are often only found in ancient remnants. Centuries of woodland cover will produce a distinctive woodland soil required by specialist plants and fungi. It is almost impossible to artificially recreate such soils, and so newly planted woods will be comparatively poor in species.

Without knowing it, many of us are able to identify an ancient woodland. When we walk through a woodland full of trees of great age and vigorous young saplings, through sunlit glades, noisy with birdsong and buzzing with insects, we instinctively recognise it as an attractive and valuable place. In many cases this is because it is an ancient woodland.

Turn left down this lane.

Bowsey Hill is situated on London Clay. After deposition of the Reading Beds, the whole area was flooded from the east by the sea, when the London Clay was laid down. As the sea advanced and deepened, it deposited a thin pebble bed of flint. This was followed by brown loamy sand with thin layers of clay and limestone containing shell and plant debris. As the sea deepened, the main layer of the London Clay (a blue-grey marine clay) accumulated on the ocean floor. Molluscs, bivalves, gastropods, crabs, fishes and sea urchins lived in the sea floor sediments. The clay becomes increasingly sandy towards the top as the sea once again receded and the upper part of the clay weathered brown.

After re-entering the woods, keep to the main track, which runs to the left at each of the junctions you encounter, eventually reaching Star Lane once more. Turn right and follow the lane down to the end of the walk.

Notice the great banks and ditches separating the track from the woods. In places the distance from ditch bottom to bank top is over six feet. In the past these banks would have been thrown up to indicate the boundary of Cayton Park. The ditches would also serve an important function in providing surface drainage from the track which, because of the clay soil, is always liable to become muddy, or worse, in wet weather.

Just before reaching Star Lane you will notice signs warning of quarry workings nearby. The area below the wood on the right holds large deposits of clay, and from here the nearby tile factory takes its materials. When clay was being extracted in the 1960s, traces of an ancient settlement were found. It may be that a small farmstead, worked by a couple of families, occupied the site until about AD 50. With the arrival of the Romans in southern Britain, and with them a new system of administration and taxation, the site appears to have been abandoned – perhaps with the families moving to a new, more stylish, Roman villa on a nearby site.

HOW TO GET THERE

By Car

Knowl Hill lies on the A4 between Twyford and Maidenhead. Park in the large lay-by outside the Seven Stars.

By Bus

The Wycombe Bus Company service No. 317 between Reading and Maidenhead on weekdays and

Saturdays, and Reading Transport service X1 between Reading and London, stop at the lay-by at Knowl Hill.

REFRESHMENTS

The Seven Stars public house at Knowl Hill and the Dew Drop Inn at Ashley Hill.

TELEPHONE

Public payphones are found in the villages of Hare Hatch and Littlewick Green either side of Knowl Hill on the A4.

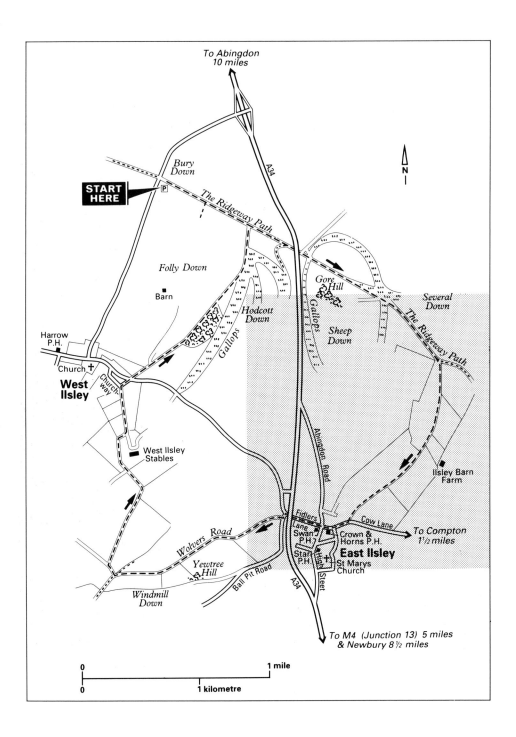

To Abingdon
10 miles

Bury
Down

START HERE P

The Ridgeway Path

A34

Folly Down

■ Barn

Gore
Hill

Several
Down

The Ridgeway Path

Hodcott
Down

Gallops

Gallops

Sheep
Down

Harrow
P.H.

Church †

Church way

**West
Ilsley**

West Ilsley
Stables

Abingdon Road

Ilsley Barn
Farm

N

Wolvers Road

Yewtree
Hill

Ball Pit Road

Windmill
Down

Fidlers
Lane

Swan
P.H.

Star
P.H.

High Steet

Cow Lane

Crown &
Horns P.H.

East Ilsley

St Marys
Church

To Compton
1½ miles

A34

To M4 (Junction 13) 5 miles
& Newbury 8½ miles

0
1 mile

0
1 kilometre

WALK TEN:
EAST/WEST ILSLEY 5 MILES

The patterns of cropped and ploughed fields, woodland, and gallops create an almost abstract image. The white chalk tracks stand out clearly, their flowing lines and curves reflecting the gentle swell of the Downs.

INTRODUCTION

The route has been described from the public car park on Bury Down, although car parking is also available in both East and West Ilsley. It is about $5\frac{1}{2}$ miles long and takes about $3\frac{1}{2}$ hours to complete. The walk follows the ancient Ridgeway across the top of the Downs and descends to the villages of East and West Ilsley, both of which grew up closely associated with the traffic passing by on the hills above them.

The Berkshire Downs' gently undulating landscape is a result of the underlying chalk, a soft white porous limestone composed mainly of the skeletons of floating marine organisms. Because it is so porous, rainfall is easily absorbed and so does not flow across the land surface causing erosion. While surrounding land has been worn down by erosion, chalk outcrops generally form areas of high ground and are found in a wide band across southern England. Bury Down is just a part of a continuous area of chalk upland spreading from the Dorset Coast to East Anglia.

Bury Down is a splendid vantage point and gives extensive views northwards across the Thames Valley and the Vale of the White Horse. In this largely agricultural scene two large establishments stand out. The northern group of buildings is the Atomic Energy Research Establishment at Harwell.

The eastern complex is the Didcot Power Station, which is coal-fired and consumes some six million tons of coal annually. The 375-ft high cooling towers were built in two groups in order to lessen their impact upon the landscape!

> Ilsley remote amidst the Berkshire Downs
> Claims those distinctions o'er her sister towns
> Far famed for sheep and wool though not for spinners
> For sportsmen, doctors, publicans and sinners.

(From Humphrey's *Berkshire book of song, rhyme and steeple chime*.)

THE WALK

Start eastwards and follow the Ridgeway to Gore Hill.

The line of the Ridgeway is here clear to see. The wide grass track, which can be used by walkers, riders and vehicles, draws a strong line across the crest of the Downs. The Ridgeway has been called England's oldest road, and though there is some uncertainty it is thought that it originated in the Bronze Age more than 3,000 years ago. Over the centuries many different people have used the track as a thoroughfare for trade between remoter parts of south-west England, East Anglia and the Midlands, while the invading armies of the Danes may have found it convenient for their forays against King Alfred in the ninth century. At that time the route may have been less clearly defined on the ground; it was not until the eighteenth and nineteenth centuries

that the track's width was specified. In the parish of West Ilsley in 1828 the width was set at 68 ft which reflected its use as a Drovers' Way.

At Gore Hill follow the track through the underpass beneath the A34 and continue along the Ridgeway.

At Gore Hill the A34 Southampton to Manchester trunk road crosses the Ridgeway. This has been a notorious spot for travellers for many years. In 1830 the Southampton coach from Oxford 'was enclosed so fast in snow at Gore Hill the coachman and passengers were necessitated to leave it'. One hundred and fifty years later the snows of the 1981/82 winter also provoked drivers to abandon their vehicles in favour of the warmth and shelter of the pubs and schoolhouses of East Ilsley. In 1986/87 a new section of dual carriageway was built at Gore Hill. An underpass was provided to remove the need for Ridgeway users to cross this busy road. After you pass through the tunnel the village of East Ilsley lies to your right in a fold of the Downs.

At the next waymark turn right down a bridleway which runs alongside some training gallops.

The Berkshire Downs around Compton, East and West Ilsley and Lambourn are scattered with variously shaped and sized strips of evenly mown grass. From the air the hills look as if they have been written on in a giant hand using an unknown alphabet. These are the training gallops used by the racehorse training industry so important in this area. The porous chalk produces soils which drain easily,

Opposite: One of the numerous old tracks leading up onto the Ridgeway

137

dry out quickly and grow a springy turf which is an ideal surface upon which to train racehorses. For similar reasons many racecourses are located on chalk downs (e.g., Epsom and Brighton) where they are less subject to cancellation due to wet weather. Horse-racing on the Downs became popular at the same time that fox-hunting was becoming fashionable in the eighteenth century, although there had been hunting on the Downs long before this. At this time the Duke of Cumberland (brother to George II) had a stables and race-track at Gore Hill, although both have been destroyed. Today there are five stables in the East and West Ilsley area involved in racehorse training, and lines of horses can often be seen walking to or from the gallops to exercise.

Follow the track down towards East Ilsley and at the end of the way turn right into the village.

The village of East Ilsley has many interesting features, of which perhaps the most immediately noticeable is the duck pond, soon to be restored. Beside the pond is the winding mechanism for the village well, long since disused. Above the village stands the church of St Mary, said to have been built by Canute in the eleventh century. Most of the present church is thirteenth century, with a belltower added in the fourteenth century, containing a peal of five bells dating from 1589.

The houses of East Ilsley Hall and Kennet House are the grandest in the village. Pevsner calls the Hall 'quite a swagger early Georgian house'. Kennet House, with six bays and a shell hood on carved brackets, dates from about 1700.

The track up on to
Hodcott Down

There has been a settlement at East Ilsley since
at least Saxon times and the numerous tracks which
lead to it, many from the Ridgeway to the north,
indicate the considerable traffic which it attracted
in the past. This was a result of the sheep fair for
which the village, once known as Market Ilsley,

was famous. This market was established by the lord of the manor during the reigns of Henry III and Edward I and was soon so prosperous as to take trade from the King's market at Wallingford. East Ilsley was ideally positioned close to the Ridgeway along which many cattle and sheep were driven to market. The market was held once or twice a month, and at its height during the eighteenth century over 80,000 sheep were penned in one day and 56,000 sold, with an annual average of 400,000 animals. With the exception of Smithfield it was the greatest sheep market in England, and was involved in the process of fattening sheep for the London market. Wool fairs were also held.

A stone plaque recording the village's former importance is to be found on a grass verge beside the road in the High Street.

Take some time to explore the village before returning to pass under the A34 road-bridge. Take the track opposite (Wolvers Road) which runs up a gentle slope away from the road.

The hill which this green lane traverses is known as Windmill Down. Years ago a windmill once stood on the road between East and West Ilsley. During a violent storm the mill was destroyed, never to be rebuilt.

At the next path junction turn right onto a bridleway which passes West Ilsley Stables. After passing the stables, turn left onto a metalled road and follow it to West Ilsley. At the road junction turn left if you wish to explore the village.

Practice jumps beside
the Ridgeway, high
above East Ilsley

West Ilsley lies in a hollow in the middle of the
Downs. Although in summer the hilltops can be calm
and hot, in winter they are bleak exposed places
where the wind is always noticeable, often strong
and biting. For this reason most of the downland

villages are found sheltered in folds of lower land out of the blast of the winter winds, in many cases at a place where a spring or well provided a source of water for the villagers. In Saxon times, West Ilsley also had a large market just to the north of the village, but it never reached the importance of its neighbour to the east.

The village contains a shop, public house, and public telephone, and is worth a short diversion.

To continue the walk cross the road and take the track up out of the village across Hodcott Down towards the Ridgeway.

On reaching the track on the Ridgeway, turn left to return to the car park at Bury Down.

HOW TO GET THERE

By Car

East and West Ilsley are reached from the A34 north of Newbury. To find the Bury Down car park, leave the A34 at the East/West Ilsley turn off, take the road to West Ilsley, and in the middle of the village turn northwards onto the road to Chilton/Didcot and follow it to the hilltop.

By Bus

Bennett's Coaches run service B34 from Newbury to West Ilsley. Tel. Chieveley (0635) 248423

REFRESHMENTS

There are three public houses in the centre of East Ilsley village. West Ilsley offers one public house, overlooking a pond and the cricket ground at the far west end of the village.

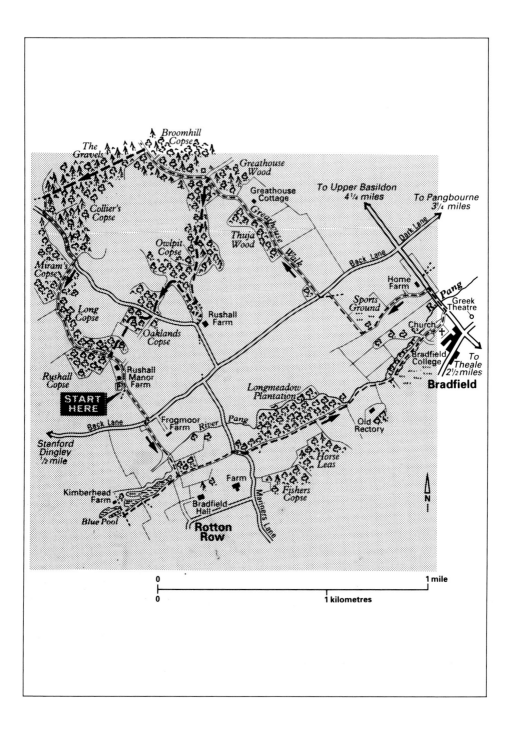

START HERE

Bradfield

Rotton
Row

To Upper Basildon
4¼ miles

To Pangbourne
3¾ miles

To
Theale
2½ miles

Stanford
Dingley
½ mile

Broomhill
Copse

The
Gravels

Greathouse
Wood

Greathouse
Cottage

Collier's
Copse

Owlpit
Copse

Thuja
Wood

Greathouse Walk

Back Lane

Dark Lane

R. Pang

Greek
Theatre

Home
Farm

Sports
Ground

Church

Bradfield
College

Miram's
Copse

Long
Copse

Oaklands
Copse

Rushall
Farm

Rushall
Copse

Rushall
Manor
Farm

Back Lane

Frogmoor
Farm

River   Pang

Longmeadow
Plantation

Old
Rectory

Horse
Leas

Fishers
Copse

Farm

Kimberhead
Farm

Bradfield
Hall

Blue Pool

Manners Lane

N

0 _____ 1 mile

0 _____ 1 kilometres

WALK ELEVEN:
BRADFIELD

4 MILES

The woods in the top half of the picture are part of a large body of woodland on the high ground west of Reading. The grounds of Bradfield Hall (bottom centre) are notable for the huge parkland trees.

INTRODUCTION

The walk is about $4\frac{1}{2}$ miles long and should take about $2\frac{1}{2}$ hours, but can be extended to $5\frac{1}{4}$ miles and approximately 3 hours. The walk has been described in an anti-clockwise direction from the car park at Rushall Manor Farm. The walk follows the River Pang into the fascinating village of Bradfield, as well as passing through some of the large areas of woodland which clothe the valley sides.

Much of the land through which you will walk is part of Rushall Farm, owned by W. Cumber & Son (Theale) Ltd. It is a 283 ha (700 acres) mixed farm with a flock of 800 sheep. The farm produces wheat, barley, oil seed rape, lamb and wool. There is also 40 ha (100 acres) of woodland. The farm encourages visitors under the auspices of the John Simonds Trust, which is an educational charity working with young people in the countryside. The Old Manor Farm has some historic buildings, including the large eighteenth-century barn beside the car park, and is now used for both exhibits and school activities. During lambing time groups are encouraged to tour the lambing sheds. The farm has other open days throughout the year; telephone Bradfield 744547 for details.

THE WALK

Walk south down the bridleway to the road (Back Lane). Turn right, then left on to the next bridleway, which leads down to a gate. Go through this and cross the bridge over the River Pang. Follow the path across a meadow by the river to reach another gate and path junction.

Turn right here, if you wish to take the opportunity to visit the famous Blue Pool and watercress beds.

The walk to the Blue Pool takes you past some old overgrown watercress beds. These provide areas of shallow water which are good breeding sites for invertebrates, which in turn attract feeding birds. The Blue Pool almost certainly derives its colourful properties from the fine particles of a mineral called glauconite, which is blue-green in colour and transmits or reflects light reaching it in the fine sands on the bed of the pool. There is a nominal charge to view the pool, and an explanatory leaflet is available on site.

The main walk turns left at the junction near the river and passes below Bradfield Hall.

Bradfield Hall dates from about 1700, but was largely built in 1763 for the Hon. John Barrington, the natural son of George II.

The footpath meets Mariners Lane. Turn right along it for about 50 yards, then left on to the next footpath, which runs along the edge of Longmeadow Plantation before rejoining the River Pang.

The Pang, with its waters flowing quickly over a chalk base, is well-suited to the breeding of trout, many of which can be seen patiently lying in wait for passing prey. The banks are lined with many varieties of water plants and trees, making a good place to watch out for birds.

Follow the path along the river, until the drive of St Andrew's parish church is reached as you enter Bradfield village.

St Andrew's was altered and added to in 1848, although there has been a church on this site since the twelfth century. The north aisle is of the fourteenth century and the tower of the sixteenth. Much of the later building is of local flint and chalk, and the oak beams and pews are from trees felled in the local area. A more detailed history is available in the church.

The village of Bradfield lies in the valley of the River Pang. The original village – The Broadfield – was centred on the river with its mill, church and manor house. Since the college has come to dominate the village, the major residential part of the parish has grown up elsewhere on higher ground at Southend.

Walk down the drive to the road: on the left can be seen the old mill and some delightful riverside cottages. Before continuing on the walk it is well worth turning right up the road to take a look at the many impressive and interesting buildings in Bradfield village.

Opposite: The River Pang as it flows into Bradfield

Bradfield is dominated by the college, a private boys' school. It was founded in 1850 by Thomas Stevens, Rector and Lord of the Manor of Bradfield, and by all accounts a remarkable man. Bradfield was among the earliest of the Victorian school foundations. Stevens wished to establish a kind of small cathedral, and, having virtually rebuilt the parish church, he desired a choir of gentlemen's sons after the fashion of Magdalen College, Oxford. The college was called St Andrew's as its first prospectus, describing an education on true church principles concentrating on the three R's as well as music, classics, history and maths, was issued on St Andrew's Day 1848. The first pupils were educated in the sixteenth-century manor house, Bradfield Place, on the north side of the church.

Apart from periods of financial difficulty in the late nineteenth century the college has steadily grown and its buildings have taken over most of the village. Their brick and flint construction provides an attractive continuity to the village architecture. The principal entrance to the college is from the Southend Road, through the large half-timbered archway. Look out for the unusual weather vane on the college chapel, which depicts a schoolmaster in cap and gown. The most famous feature of the village is the Greek Theatre, formed from an abandoned chalk pit in the 1880s. Accommodating nearly 2,000 specators, the theatre was based on the amphitheatre at Epidaurus and has been the venue for a cycle of Greek plays at Bradfield since 1890.

(The route description continues from the point at which the track from the church reaches the road.)

Turn left at the road and walk along as far as the next wide track on the left. Turn left down the track. At the next stile the walk continues along the track passing below the college cricket ground. Cross the next stile and turn right to follow the field edge up to Back Lane. Cross the road and walk up the track opposite, known as Greathouse Walk, which climbs the valley side.

Just beyond Greathouse Cottages a large grass mound will be seen on the right. This is a covered water reservoir, and supplies some of the local farms.

At the reservoir a choice can be made; for a longer walk omit the following three paragraphs.

For a shorter walk, turn left off the track and follow the path down through the woods, in which some large pine trees can be seen. The path emerges from the wood at a stile. Cross over, and follow the field edge to the next stile and then back into the wood. Here the walk leaves the public right of way and follows a nature trail which the landowner has created as a Permitted Path. Please follow the path, keeping between the white posts.

The woodland through which the walk passes is varied and contains a wide range of plants usually only found in woodlands of great age. Wood anemone and yellow archangel are two flowers which are only found in undisturbed ground, so their presence here indicates that the land has never been ploughed.

The path crosses Scratchface Lane, and emerges back at the farm and the end of the walk.
   To extend the walk, carry on up Greathouse Walk.

To the right of the track you have just walked is Greathouse Wood. This is named after the brand new mansion built by a London merchant who had found the decaying Bradfield Place, the original manor house of the parish, uninhabitable. However, this new mansion has now totally disappeared, leaving only the name of the woodland as a reminder of its existence.

Turn left onto the next footpath.

This path runs through a wood which is mainly of fir. Although the path is here very close to the M4 the thick woodland deadens the traffic noise to a great extent. Wildlife has quickly grown accustomed to the nearby motorway and deer footprints (cleavers) and sometimes deer themselves, roe or muntjak, may be seen on the path.

The path emerges from the wood at a field. Cross the stile and turn left to follow the field edge to Scratchface Lane. Turn left through the gate and walk down the lane for about 400 yards.

The lane is fairly narrow, but at least today it is not as painful to negotiate as its name indicates it was in the past. You can imagine carters fending off the lashes of bramble stems growing out from the hedgebanks, as they jolted down the hill towards the farm below. On the banks beside the lane, particularly in

Opposite: Riverside cottages at Bradfield

the spring and summer, wild flowers can be seen, as well as evidence of the presence of rabbits, voles and mice.

Turn right off the road onto the bridleway.

This path passes through woods which the evidence of eighteenth-century maps suggests have been in existence since before 1600. They are probably remnants of the wild wood which used to cover this country. Their great age is reflected in the wide variety of plants and animals which can be found in them. For centuries these woods had a vital role to play in the life of the farm. The trees supplied valuable products such as firewood, fence poles and timber for the construction of everything from gates to farm buildings. Some of these were produced by coppicing the trees – a management system which involved cutting down the stems of deciduous trees on a cycle which produced regular crops of evenly sized poles. In the years after cutting the tender new shoots are very vulnerable to browsing by deer, so the woods were often surrounded by ditches and banks surmounted by hedges. This helped to keep the deer out, and the banks, sometimes with thorn tree remnants of the hedges on top of them, can still be seen in and around many old coppice woodlands today.

The bridleway leads back to the farm and the end of the walk.

HOW TO GET THERE

By Car

A car park is soon to be provided at Rushall Manor Farm, which is reached along Back Lane from Bradfield, best approached along the minor road leading off the A340 Theale to Pangbourne road. If the car park at Rushall Manor Farm is unavailable there are other informal pull-ins beside the road in and around Bradfield.

By Bus

The Bee Line Bus Company service 101 between Newbury, Thatcham, Theale and Reading stops at Bradfield College. Tel. Reading 581358 or Newbury 40743 for timetable information.

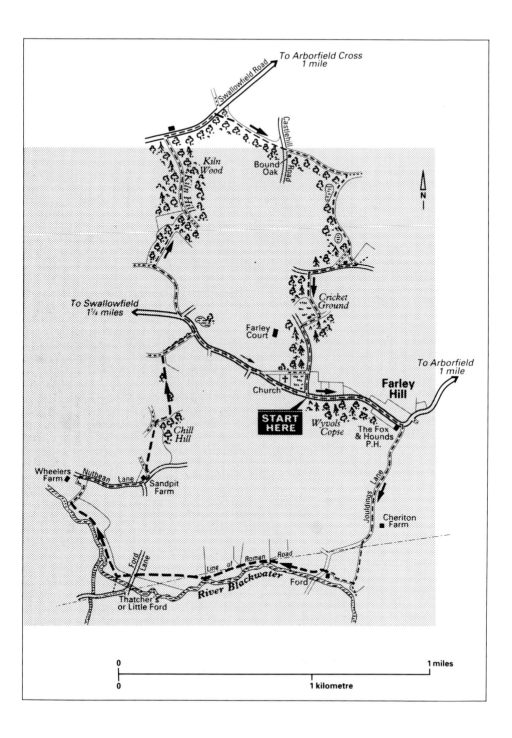

To Arborfield Cross
1 mile

Swallowfield Road

Castlehill Road

Kiln Wood

Kiln Hill

Bound Oak

N

To Swallowfield
1¼ miles

Farley Court

Cricket Ground

To Arborfield
1 mile

Church

FARLEY HILL

START HERE

Wyvols Copse

The Fox & Hounds P.H.

Chill Hill

Wheelers Farm

Nuthean Lane

Sandpit Farm

Jouldings Lane

Cheriton Farm

Ford Lane

Line of Roman Road

River Blackwater

Ford

Thatcher's or Little Ford

0		1 miles
0	1 kilometre	

WALK TWELVE:
FARLEY HILL

4 MILES

The sinuous line of the River Blackwater is easily seen in this photo, taken when the river was in full flow. The open fields of the valley sides contrast with the heavily wooded hilltop where the village is located.

INTRODUCTION

The walk is about $4\frac{1}{2}$ miles long and should take approximately $2\frac{1}{2}$ hours, but can be shortened to $2\frac{1}{2}$ miles and $1\frac{3}{4}$ hours. The walk has been described in a clockwise direction from the T-junction near the church in the village centre.

Farley Hill is a scattered hamlet standing on high ground in the south-east corner of the parish of Swallowfield. Among its woods and copses are some impressive buildings, such as Farley Hill Place, Farley Castle and Farley Court. Although of these three you are only likely to get a glimpse of the latter, and that from a distance, there are other attractive buildings to be seen along the route. The walk leads through contrasting scenery of open fields and shady lanes and woods.

THE WALK

Walk eastwards through the village to the Fox and Hounds public house. Turn right here and walk down Jouldings Lane.

This easily overlooked part of Berkshire owes its attractive landscape to the presence of an outcrop of plateau gravel rising above the valley of the River

Blackwater. The prominent wooded hilltop of Farley Hill features in countryside views from large parts of the surrounding area. For this reason the local authority, Wokingham District Council, has designated it an Area of Special Landscape Importance. This enables local planners to protect the location from development which would detract from its attractive rural character and special landscape qualities. Farley Hill has considerably more woodland than much of the surrounding countryside because its soils are derived from gravel and clay and are thus either too poor or too wet for agriculture. These woodlands are a mixture of natural copses of great age which are rich in wildlife, and more recent plantations; the walk will lead you through several different types, with their varied wildlife communities.

After passing Cheriton Farm, cross the stile on the left and follow the path along the field edge. At the next path junction turn right over the stile and follow the path back to Jouldings Lane. Turn left down the lane for a short distance to the river.

Jouldings Lane terminates here at a ford. Although the river is small there are no bridges across it between Eversley to the east and Swallowfield to the west, but there are three fords. Although usable by large agricultural vehicles, these fords present a barrier to normal through traffic, and effectively turn both Jouldings and Ford Lanes into culs-de-sac. This leads to comparative isolation for those who live in the nearby cottages and farms, but has helped to retain the area's rural appeal.

The Broadwater
flowing to join the
River Loddon

The River Blackwater is surprisingly modest in
size considering the breadth of the valley in which it
lies. Originally it was much larger, its headwaters
lying further to the south beyond the Hog's Back on
the North Downs. Gradual downward erosion of the

land's surface allowed the River Wey to capture these headwaters, leaving the Blackwater as a 'misfit' which is seldom significant in the valley it follows.

Walk back up the lane from the ford and turn left onto a path opposite the one used earlier. Follow this path alongside the River Blackwater, although it does not always follow the river's course.

In earlier times the valley would have been considerably wetter and more marshy and would have been virtually uninhabitable. The Blackwater Valley as a whole is characterised by large amounts of scrubland and rough pasture, while in the valley floor there are few really large trees or areas of woodland. This contrasts strongly with the major blocks of woodland on either slope of the valley's sides: Forestry Commission pine plantations to the south and mixed deciduous and coniferous woodlands to the north.

Cross several fields before ending at Ford Lane.

As the name suggests, there is a ford on the river at this point. There is still evidence of terracing where a Roman road, which ran from Silchester via Staines to London, crossed the river. This road formed part of a major route which continued westwards to Bristol and the West Country. Unlike many other Roman roads, this one, locally known as The Devil's Highway, did not remain an important long-distance route after Roman influence declined. When the town of Silchester was destroyed during the Saxon invasion the Roman road was abandoned, and gradually travellers chose to pass through what are now Reading and Maidenhead, roughly along the line of today's A4. So while other Roman roads have been built up and are today used by modern traffic, the Devil's Highway is mostly little more than a track frequented by walkers and horse-riders.

Cross the lane and the path returns to run alongside the river.

The River Blackwater is soon joined by the Whitewater, flowing in from the south. After their confluence the river is called the Broadwater and flows north-westwards to where it joins the River Loddon near Swallowfield. The Blackwater and Whitewater rivers are said to have been named as a result of the colour of the sediment which they carry in times of flood. The Whitewater drains off chalk country, while the Blackwater has its source among peaty heathland soils. Both rivers are subject to periods of low flow during summer and hence are vulnerable to pollution, especially where the Blackwater flows through the heavily built-up areas near Farnborough. In this stretch the waters are fairly free of contamination and are regularly fished by anglers.

Continue along the path beside the river, then turn away towards Wheelers Farm to end at Nutbean Lane. Turn right along the lane. At Sandpit Farm turn left onto the track, then go through the gate and follow the path up the hill. Cross the stile, turn right and follow the field edge until the path turns left to cross the field down to the track. Turn right onto the track, and where this ends at a road a choice can be made.

For the short walk, turn right and follow the road back to the village.

For the longer walk, turn left. At the next road junction take the grassy track opposite.

This walk follows a number of green lanes – lanes which are for the most part grassy tracks flanked by hedges. As well as being attractive to walk and ride along, they are important sites for wildlife, as they often provide a refuge for plants and animals which find the surrounding farmland inhospitable. The shelter provided by the hedges may make part of the lanes damper or warmer than the more exposed fields nearby, and so provide variety in an area's habitats. They provide good feeding areas for bats which feed on insect species associated with mature hedgerows, while the hedge-bottom is home to mammals such as woodmice, bank voles and shrews, which search for seeds and invertebrates among the leaf litter and low branches. These small mammals in turn provide food for birds of prey such as kestrels or owls which hunt along the lanes. Some may once have been important routes for local people to use in their daily lives but now, while traffic speeds by on other roads, here one may walk or ride at leisure in peaceful seclusion.

Turn right at the path junction and on reaching the Kiln Hill track, turn left.

Woodland names can give an indication of their past use or history. Some may take the name of the parish or village, others the name of a family who owned the wood and used it for household fuel,

while others reflect some previous industrial use. The wood on the right is Kiln Wood, which in the past may have supplied fuel for the nearby brick-works. Similarly, there is a sandpit nearby which has given its name to the local farm and lane, so it must once have been of some importance. Woodland names sometimes change over the years. In the nineteenth century Kiln Wood was known as Upper and Lower Mossland Copse, while the three nearby woods, Rapleys Shaw, Rapleys Shaw Coppice and First Close Coppice, have now become New Plantation.

Turn right at Swallowfield Road and then right down the next bridleway. Cross Castle Hill Road and take the track opposite.

At the road junction stands the Bound Oak. The local name of this ancient tree probably derives from its position on the boundary between the parishes of Arborfield and Newland, and Swallowfield. It has been pollarded in the past, a management technique which can prolong a tree's life. To pollard a tree its branches are cut from the trunk at a height of 10 or 12 ft and then allowed to regrow. This is very much like coppicing, except that it is at the top of the tree's trunk rather than at its base. Pollarding produces repeated crops of vigorous young growth while the trunk supporting them continues to age. If the pollard is cut regularly, the weight of the new growth never becomes insupportable, and while other aged trees may split apart from the weight of their huge branches a pollard can live on for centuries. In the

Opposite: The path rising from Sandpit Lane to Chill Hill

Kiln Hill passing down
through Kiln Wood

markers. Although the tree has many dead branches, this does not necessarily mean that the tree is dying. Oak trees which look like this may be quite healthy and live on for many years. It is because oaks are rarely allowed to live into old age and are usually felled quite early in their lives that we are unused to seeing them in this form. The giant, aged oaks of Windsor Great Park are splendid examples of the gnarled and contorted shapes which trees can develop if allowed to live into their old age. The rotting branches provide roosting sites for bats and both nesting and feeding sites for birds. Mature trees such as this are therefore important for wildlife.

Continue along the track. At a bridleway junction turn right and follow the bridleway to the road. Turn right and then shortly left down the path which runs past the cricket ground. Turn right and then left at the road junction and walk down the road to the walk's starting point.

HOW TO GET THERE

By Car

Located away from major routes, Farley Hill is not terribly easy to find. The best way to reach the village centre is probably along the minor road which runs between the A327 Arborfield Cross to Eversley road and Swallowfield.

By Bus

The Bee Line service 141 from Wokingham to Farley Hill Court, Wednesday and Friday only. Tel. Reading 581358 for timetable details.

REFRESHMENTS

The Fox and Hounds public house in Farley Hill village.

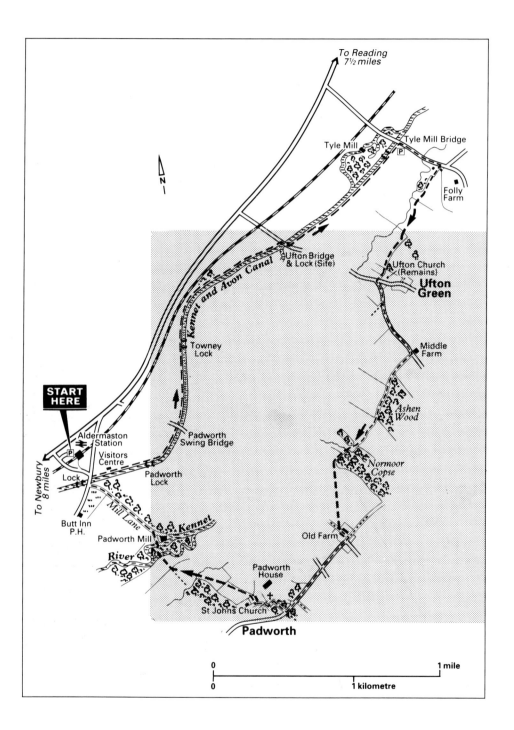

To Reading
7½ miles

Tyle Mill

Tyle Mill Bridge

P

Folly
Farm

Kennet and Avon Canal

Ufton Bridge
& Lock (Site)

Ufton Church
(Remains)

**Ufton
Green**

Towney
Lock

Middle
Farm

N

**START
HERE**

*Ashen
Wood*

Aldermaston
Station

P

Padworth
Swing Bridge

*Normoor
Copse*

Visitors
Centre

Lock

Padworth
Lock

To Newbury
8 miles

Butt Inn
P.H.

Mill Lane

Old Farm

Kennet

Padworth Mill

River

Padworth
House

St Johns Church

Padworth

0   1 mile

0   1 kilometre

168

WALK THIRTEEN:
PADWORTH

5 MILES

The importance of the Kennet valley as a transport corridor is clear from the way the railway, the Kennet and Avon Canal, and the A4 run in parallel down its centre in the top left of the picture, separated by only a few yards.

INTRODUCTION

The walk is about 5½ miles long, should take about 3 hours to complete, and has been described from the car park at Aldermaston railway station. As well as following the towpath of the Kennet and Avon Canal through a landscape of pasture and woodlands, the route climbs the southern slope of the Kennet Valley to give wider views. Aldermaston Wharf and the canal have fascinating histories. The walk passes the British Waterways Visitor Information Centre located beside the canal in a traditional eighteenth-century canalman's cottage at Lower Wharf, Padworth. Further information about the canal is available there.

THE WALK

Cross the footbridge over the railway line and walk down the short track to Aldermaston Wharf on the Kennet and Avon Canal.

In 1714 an Act of Parliament was passed to improve the navigability of the River Kennet between Reading and Newbury. This was achieved by a series of short canals bypassing the bends of the river. By 1810 the canal had been extended to link Reading with Bristol, but within 150 years the canal was closed to through traffic and facing a future as little more than a reed-filled ditch. However, the canal has now been restored by the Kennet and Avon Canal Trust and British Waterways, latterly with substantial support from Berkshire County Council and Newbury District Council, and the whole canal was re-opened to through boat traffic in 1990. Aldermaston Wharf was one of eleven wharfing points along the canal and was once exceedingly busy. The products of Berkshire's coppice woods, especially those in and around the Kennet Valley, were once in great demand. Birch trees from the commons on the high ground on either side of the valley, hazel and ash from the coppices on the slopes, and willow from the wet woodlands along the valley bottom all provided raw materials for the hoops, brooms, and round and hewn timber that was sent in large quantities to London from the wharf. Returning boats brought coal, groceries and manufactured goods. The wharf was restored by the Trust in 1983. The canal spur to the north of Aldermaston Lock was once longer and used to link the canal with the railway so that goods could be transferred from one to the other.

Walk to the left along the towpath, passing on your right the cottages below Aldermaston Wharf and the recently rebuilt Padworth Lock and Padworth Swing Bridge.

After its completion the canal only enjoyed a short period of prosperity. It had been constructed at the end of the canal building era, and soon had to compete with the railway, at this point running parallel with it down the Kennet Valley. In 1852 the canal was bought by the Great Western Railway, but its fortunes declined until by the 1950s sections had become so dangerous that they were closed and through traffic became impossible. The last commercial barge sailed in 1951. Padworth Bridge became fixed in a closed position and for some time was the limit of navigation westwards from Reading. In common with many others, the old bridge has now been replaced with a new modern construction as part of the restoration programme.

At the bridge, cross the road then follow the towpath past Towney Lock to Ufton Lock and Swing Bridge.

Ufton Lock was originally shallow, only having a rise of 1 ft 9 in. Its role was to improve the head of water below Towney Lock upstream, but when that lock was rebuilt Ufton became redundant. Its gates were removed and that is how it stands today.

On reaching the road, the path crosses to the other side of the waterway. Cross the swing bridge and then cross a stile on your left to follow the towpath beside the river.

Opposite: An invitation to rest in the shade of Padworth churchyard's giant yew

At Ufton Bridge the River Kennet joins the canal after following a more sinuous course than the canal in the centre of the valley to the south. This is a feature of the canal; stretches of man-made navigation linking together navigable and fairly direct stretches of river.

Follow the towpath to Tyle Mill.

The Mill stands among trees astride the River Kennet on a site of great antiquity. It was once owned by Reading Abbey, and may have existed before the Norman Conquest. Originally it was a corn mill, but in 1914 the building burned down and was replaced by a saw mill. Now it is a private residence.

Turn right at the road. Walk up the road for a short distance, then turn right onto the footpath (opposite a road junction). This path runs alongside a house and then passes out into old meadows.

As the path rises, views across the Kennet Valley to the north open up. Flanked to north and south by higher land made of London Clays, the valley contains rich deposits of sand and gravel. While every effort is made to limit the impact of such activity, the demands of the construction industry mean that over the years some of these minerals will be gradually extracted. In the meantime the view is a peaceful agricultural scene punctuated by plantations of poplar trees which flourish in the damp conditions of the valley bottom.

Just before the road is reached, on the left you will see the ivy-covered remains of the church of Ufton Richard, a parish which no longer exists. It was founded by the Brethren of the Order of St John of Jerusalem in 1338 but was closed in 1435 when St Peter's, higher up the hill in Ufton Nervet, became the local parish church. The old church was later converted into two cottages, which were demolished in 1886.

The path ends at a road junction where a restored cattle pound stands on a small green. Walk up the lane opposite the path until you reach Middle Farm. Turn right onto the farm track.

On your left is Ashen Wood, an ancient wood which is one of the few sites in Berkshire that has the 'bottle sedge' among its floral rarities.

At the next path junction go straight across the meadow, keeping the hedge on your left. The path passes alongside Normoor Copse. At the end of the copse the path runs diagonally uphill to Old Farm. Walk through the farmyard and at the road turn right. Go straight across at the crossroads.

On 21 September 1643 Robert Devereux, 3rd Earl of Essex, and his Parliamentarian soldiers were passing through this area on their way to London after the Battle of Newbury, when they were attacked by Royalist cavalry led by Prince Rupert. The Royalists were at first overpowering and some of the Parliamentarian soldiers ran, shouting that all was lost. However, Essex rallied his men, spreading them along the hedges on either side of the lane. After a short but bloody skirmish the Royalists were forced to disengage, losing, it is said, some three hundred men. Essex's wearied troops pushed on eastwards to Theale, where they quartered for the night. This was the last action of the Battle of Newbury.

Turn right at the sign for Padworth Church, and walk down the lane.

Padworth Church stands strangely isolated from the largest settlement in the parish, located at the road, rail and canal intersection at Aldermaston Wharf. It is said that the medieval village of Padworth, which stood around the church, was destroyed by the Black Death in the fourteenth century. The village must have stood full in the path of the pestilence as it swept towards London from its source in the West Country. With the inhabitants dead the village decayed leaving no trace of any dwellings, and when settlers returned they chose not to rebuild on the contaminated site.

The church of St John the Baptist is one of the best examples of a pure Norman church and dates from about 1130. It is built of rendered flint with corners formed of square stone blocks. Like a lot of churches in the quieter parts of Berkshire, the nave has several wall paintings, including a depiction of St Nicholas, and beneath him the 'Miracle of the Three Boys'. The bellcote is supported on massive timbers and contains six bells, five of which were recast during the restoration of the church in 1890. The inscriptions on the original bells were reproduced on the new ones. That on the third bell reads '*Sancta Maria Ora Pro Nobis*', and on the tenor bell 'Henri Knight made me 1597'.

Behind the church is Padworth House. It is a typical Adam building of the eighteenth century and probably occupies the site of the old manor house. The house is now a college but still enjoys fine views over a lightly wooded park and the valley beyond.

At the War Memorial outside the church, turn left and follow the path round the church boundary,

Opposite: Padworth War Memorial and church

passing through the gate, and continue on towards a house. Turn right onto the path that passes between the house and some farm buidings. Follow the way-marks down through fields, crossing some small footbridges on your way. The path leads to the River Kennet and Padworth Mill.

Padworth Mill, which dates back to 1690, lies on an island formed by the mill-stream and the river. Well before the construction of the canal, there would have been many mills employing the water power of the River Kennet; a mill here was mentioned in the Domesday Book. When plans for the construction of the canal were drawn up it would have been a prime concern to ensure that these mills did not lose their water supply. The public rights of way through the mill cross over several footbridges, and at certain times of the year, the water underneath the bridges seem to boil with trout.

After the last footbridge, the path runs between a chain-link fence and a row of cypress trees. At the end of this path turn left onto Mill Lane. Follow the lane back to Aldermaston Wharf and the end of the walk.

HOW TO GET THERE

By Car

British Rail have kindly allowed the use of the Aldermaston Station car park. This is signposted from the A4 travelling westwards between Theale and Newbury. A new car park is also being constructed beside the canal at Tyle Mill which will be reached by turning off the A4 closer to Theale.

By Bus

The Bee Line Bus Company service 102/103 between Reading and Newbury stops at Aldermaston Station (Monday to Saturday). On Sundays the service is provided by Reading Buses.

By Train

British Rail runs an excellent rail service from Monday to Saturday between Reading Central Station and Newbury stopping at Aldermaston: Tel. Reading 595911 or Newbury 40656 for timetable information.

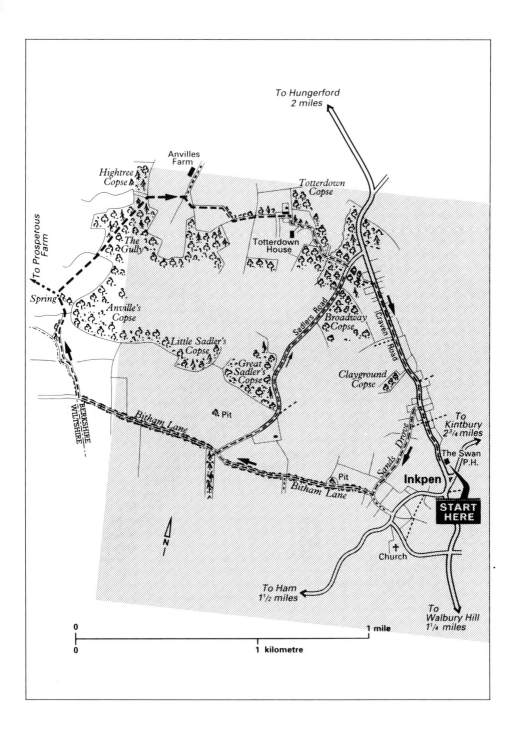

To Hungerford
2 miles

Anvilles Farm

Hightree Copse

Totterdown Copse

The Gully

Totterdown House

To Prosperous Farm

Spring

Anville's Copse

Broadway Copse

Sadlers Road

Craven Road

Little Sadler's Copse

Great Sadler's Copse

Clayground Copse

Pit

BERKSHIRE WILTSHIRE

Bitham Lane

To Kintbury 2¾ miles

The Swan P.H.

Sands Drove

Inkpen

Pit

Bitham Lane

START HERE

N

Church

To Ham 1½ miles

To Walbury Hill 1¼ miles

0   1 mile

0   1 kilometre

WALK FOURTEEN:
INKPEN

2 MILES

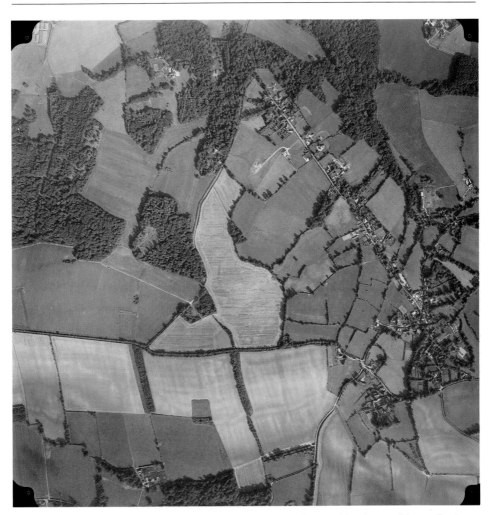

See how this part of Inkpen village straggles out along the road leading to Hungerford, and how the tiny irregularly shaped fields close to the village contrast with the large square or rectangular ones further away.

INTRODUCTION

The walk is about $2\frac{1}{2}$ miles long and should take about $1\frac{1}{4}$ hours, but can be extended to 4 miles long and approximately 2 hours. The walk has been described in a clockwise direction from the car park at the Swan Inn, Inkpen. The inn is a Free House (closed Mondays), offering a fine selection of beers, and is mentioned in *The Good Food Guide 'Cheap Eats'* 1988/89.

Hidden away in the south-western corner of Berkshire is an area of countryside which feels quite isolated. Although only a short distance from Hungerford and the M4, the scattered villages which make up Inkpen and neighbouring West Woodhay feel somewhat cut off from the busier parts of the county. The scattered woodlands, twisting narrow lanes and undulating land combine to produce an intimate and sometimes confusing landscape. This walk will lead you through just one part of the parish; there remains much more to explore.

Turn right from the Swan car park and walk down the road to Holm Dean House. Here turn left into Sands Drove Lane.

The name Inkpen is derived from the Anglo-Saxon 'Inga's Pen'. A pen was a form of enclosure, and

Inga was the person who owned it. The village is made up of a scatter of hamlets, groups of buildings having developed at Little Common, Inkpen Great Common, Lower Green and Upper Green. These names hint at the landscape of the past, when large areas of land hereabouts were open heath of which little now remains.

The village was once a hive of industry. The names of the houses and lanes give clues to their original uses; for example, Puddle Wharf Cottage, Weavers Lane and Clayground Copse. However, Inkpen was best known for its pottery, a craft which thrived until the early years of this century. Heavy types of pot such as pitchers, bread crocks, flower and chimney pots were made from local clay. Once there were three blacksmiths and four public houses, but only two of the pubs remain in business.

The village church was founded by Roger de Ingpen, and an effigy to him stands to the right of the altar. Salisbury Cathedral has a similar carving and it is thought that they both date from around AD 1230.

Follow Sands Drove to a junction with another wide green lane.

The settlements of Inkpen and West Woodhay to the east are interconnected by a complex network of narrow lanes. Indeed, it may be hard for newcomers to the area to find their way around. As well as the numerous tarmac roads there are a similar number of other lanes which have never been made up. These often have names and form quiet routes along which to bypass the road traffic and view the village from a new perspective.

183

At the junction turn right.

This track is called Bitham Lane. It runs east-west between Inkpen and Shalbourne village, five miles away in Wiltshire, and is thought to be part of a drove road to Salisbury. Although in places it is overgrown, it is possible to see that the width of the lane between its flanking hedges is considerable. Perhaps the best time to appreciate the diversity of these hedges is late in the year, when every bush seems laden with some kind of fruit. Purple sloes, crimson haws, chains of blood-red bryony berries and the gaudy pink and orange of the spindle fruit stand out against the autumn leaves. The large number of tree and shrub species found along the lane is an indication of its age, and as you walk it is easy to feel that this lane has remained much the same while the landscape nearby has been through many changes.

Look to your left. Dominating the skyline you will see Gallows Down and Walbury Hill. At 975 ft, Walbury Hill is the highest point on the chalk in Britain and is the northernmost scarp slope of the Hampshire Downs. This chalk ridge is dotted with ancient remains. On Walbury Hill, in a commanding position overlooking the Kennet Valley to the north and the Hampshire Downs to the south, is an Iron Age hill-fort, enclosing some 82 acres. Just to the west, and standing on a large Neolithic long barrow, is Combe Gibbet. The macabre intention is plain for all to see. The original gibbet was erected in 1776 for the execution of George Broomham and his mistress Dorothy Newman. They were tried and convicted of the murder of Broomham's wife and son. Many tales

Opposite: Little Common, Inkpen

184

Sands Drove Lane,
winding along behind
Inkpen's cottages

and legends surround the gibbet, but although torn down on a number of occasions it has always been replaced, its sinister silhouette now an essential part of the scenery.

After about half a mile, a track joins Bitham Lane from the right and here a choice can be made:

For a short walk, turn right and follow the track down to Sadlers Road. Follow the lane until you see a footpath signpost on your right, just before the T-junction with the Hungerford–Inkpen road. At this signpost, cross the stile. At this point the short walk rejoins the longer walk. Go to the penultimate route instruction.

The longer walk carries on along Bitham Lane for about half a mile until a footpath sign is reached. This point is the county boundary of Berkshire and Wiltshire. Turn right at the signpost, and follow the path down to the bottom of the hill. Follow the path through a gate and into an old

meadow. In the field is a fresh-water spring: walk up the slope and slightly right towards it. Here there is a junction of footpaths.

The path to the west runs to Prosperous Farm, between 1709 and his death in 1741 the home of Jethro Tull, an important figure in the development of British agriculture. He was the author of *The Horse-Hoeing Husbandry*, a book which explained the benefits of deep (horse-powered) cultivation to the growth of crops. He invented the first seed drill ever used, which reduced the amount of seed required when sowing. Tull's ideas were far in advance of his time and were ridiculed by his contemporaries, although more appreciated in France and Scotland.

Tull also had to deal with problems among his workforce, who saw his new ideas as a threat to their livelihood. Perhaps it was this early awareness of the labour-saving nature of new methods which later made Inkpen men so active in the Swing Riots. In 1830, agriculture was in recession and farm labourers and their families were living in appalling hardship, especially on the corn-growing chalk lands such as around Inkpen. Prospects of finding winter employment in such areas were poor; the traditional occupation was threshing. The mechanisation of this task threatened the labourers' last lifeline, so when the riots broke out, the violence was largely targeted on the new threshing machines, their owners and the corn they produced.

On the nights of 22 and 23 November 1830 there were riots in Hungerford and major, well-organised outbreaks of violence in Inkpen, West Woodhay,

Kintbury and Hamstead Marshall. The Yeomanry was called out, resulting in the arrest of 100 ringleaders. Although only one was executed, many were transported or imprisoned. The countryside through which you walk is today tranquil, but for a fortnight 160 years ago it was a place of threats, intimidation and violence, followed by a retribution no less terrible.

Take the path that runs north towards a wood. Cross the stile and enter the wood. Follow the path through the wood, which can be wet in parts. When the gate is reached turn right and follow the waymarks across the fields (Anvilles Farm will be on the left) and up the hill to the stile. Cross the stile and turn left. The path then runs along the hedged field boundary. The footpath passes through what was once the kitchen garden of Totterdown House. Walk down the drive bordered by rhododendron bushes and large oaks.

In one of the numerous sand pits near here were found some notable examples of prehistoric pottery over 4,000 years old. One piece is an unusual four-legged bowl, the first of its kind to be found in Britain. Another, at $11\frac{1}{2}$ in. high, has proved to be the tallest Bronze Age beaker yet found in the British Isles. Both these finds can be seen in the Newbury Museum.

Cross Sadlers Lane and take the path opposite. This runs through an avenue of beech trees and across a field.

Opposite: Easy walking near Totterdown

This part of the village is called Little Common. The

clumps of gorse beside the path are reminders of the heathland which once covered so much of the parish.

At the end of the path you will reach a road. Turn right, and follow Craven Road through the village to the Swan Inn and the end of the walk.

WALBURY HILL AND COMBE GIBBET

Both of these sites are accessible from Inkpen on foot or by car. Rights of way lead directly to the base of the hill and then up its side to the ridge. Minor roads from Inkpen will take you to the three parking areas on the ridge from where, on a clear day, you can enjoy spectacular views over several counties, and take a closer look at the historic remains.

HOW TO GET THERE

By Car

From Hungerford take the minor road across the Common to Inkpen and continue through the village until you reach your starting point.

By Bus

Take the Bee Line Bus Co. service 113 from Newbury bus station to Inkpen via Hamstead Marshall and Kintbury. Tel. Newbury 40743 for timetable information.

REFRESHMENTS

The Swan Inn, Inkpen (closed Mondays).

TELEPHONE

There is a public payphone at the small village green just south of the Swan Inn.